Liberated Connection

Fleur Elizabeth

First published 2025 by FE-ED Pty Ltd

Produced by Independent Ink

Copyright © FE-ED Pty Ltd 2025

The moral right of the author to be identified as the author of this work has been asserted.

All rights reserved. No part of this publication may be reproduced, stored in a retrieval system or transmitted in any form or by any means available now or in the future without the prior written permission of the author, nor be otherwise circulated in any form of binding or cover other than that in which it is published and without a similar condition being imposed on the purchaser.

Cover design by Catucci Design
Edited by Christine Egner and Daina Lindeman
Internal design by Independent Ink
Typeset in Greycliff CF by Post Pre-press Group, Brisbane

ISBN 978-1-7642293-6-4 (paperback)
ISBN 978-1-7642293-7-1 (epub)
ISBN 978-1-7642293-8-8 (kindle)

To Caroline and Michelle D.

Thank you for guiding me to connect to my feminine energy and inner wisdom. You taught me to trust the universe and believe that everything unfolds for my greater good. As my mentors during such a transformative phase of my life, you made a remarkable impact.

Disclaimer

The content you're about to explore reflects a coaching approach I've carefully crafted. It draws on my experiences in performance and nutritional health coaching, combining techniques from Acceptance and Commitment Therapy (ACT), Motivational Interviewing, and Dialectical Behaviour Therapy (DBT). It's important to understand that this is a coaching program, not clinical therapy.

Please remember, the information shared here is not a substitute for advice from your doctor or therapist, including psychologists, counsellors, or psychiatrists. This book isn't meant to replace any ongoing or future therapy you may be undergoing, especially trauma therapy.

This publication is not a clinical treatment for mental health conditions such as mood disorders, eating disorders, body dysmorphia, or alcohol addiction, particularly those related to sexual violence, abuse, or mental abuse.

To be clear: The Change Experience Book Series, along with myself as the author, publisher, and creator, cannot be held responsible or liable for any effects that actions taken, or drugs used may have on your body or mental health from engaging with this material.

If, at any point, the content triggers difficult emotions or past experiences, please contact your doctor or therapist immediately. Your emotional wellbeing is my priority.

Your Free Gift

As a thank you for joining me on this journey, I have a special free gift for you. You can download it, along with other helpful resources from The Change Experience book series, by signing up to the Resources page on my website.

To get your free gift, simply visit: www.fleurelizabeth.com

Contents

Preface
Let's Recap   3
The Book Structure   8

Let's Begin
1   The Home Stretch   13
2   Change Is Not Always Easy   19
3   My Trauma Experience   23

Unpacking Your Energy
4   Navigating Your Inner Power   35
5   Good and Not-So-Good Vibrations   44
6   Hypervigilant Energy   58
7   My Trauma Experience   67
8   Yin and Yang   76
9   My Wounded Energy Experience   103
10   Connecting to Your Energy   111

Traversing Energetic Exchanges
11   Energetic Loving-Yourself-Actions   123
12   Reflection Time   137
13   Don't Give Away Your Power   141
14   My Trauma Experience   146

The Liberating Power of Boundaries
15   The Boundary Blueprint   153

The Light and Dark in All of Us
16 I'm Fine 171
17 Reflection Time 179

The Art of Intentional Creation
18 Manifesting Your Deepest Desires 187
19 Reflection Time 198

Your Liberation Toolbox 2.0
20 The Superpowers Continue 207
21 Remember When 233

Liberated Connection – A Future Defined by You
22 What's the Vibe Now? 239
23 The Triumph of You 250

Appendix and References
Your Living Blueprint 255
Your Future Self, Reimagined 259
References and Research 268

Preface

THE CHANGE EXPERIENCE
Heal your past, transform your today

Project Clarity
The trauma-informed woman: *Unmask hidden wounds, end automatic coping habits and embrace your authentic self.*

- Why I'm here
- Is this you?
- Trauma defined
- Strategies for change
- Change is hard
- Your Future Self
- Life is automatic

- Family influences
- Values – your past and future
- Living by your values
- Your relationship with food and drink
- Stress and sleep

A New Perspective
The emotionally resilient woman: *Recognise your triggers, cultivate self-acceptance and embrace emotional health.*

- Becoming friends with your emotions
- Repetitive cycles
- Searching for happiness
- Your emotions invalidated
- Adverse Childhood Experiences
- Emotional regulation
- Triggers defined

- Trigger, behaviour, consequence
- Triggers – gaslighting
- Your liberation tool kit
- How to trust yourself, self-empathy, embrace mistakes, self-acceptance
- Grounding techniques

YOU ARE HERE

Liberated Connection
The energetic woman: *Set healthy boundaries, honour your needs and embrace your feminine power.*

- Change can be tough
- Embracing your energy
- Healing hypervigiliance
- Removing chaos
- Energy Vampires
- Boundary setting

- Barriers to change
- Energetic conflict resolution
- Getting what you want in life
- S.M.A.R.T Energy focused
- Become your Future Self

I.
Let's Recap

How's Your Perspective Now?
Hello, My Friend, Welcome Back

If you're holding this book, it means you've already walked through the fire. You've been brave enough to unearth and connect with the messiest, most vulnerable parts of yourself in Book One: *Project Clarity* and Book Two: *A New Perspective*.

You didn't just dip your toes in; you got soaked with the truth of your own story. You dared to peek behind the curtain of those old, familiar patterns that kept you stuck, and you were honest enough to admit they were there. You've started to understand that those little nudges and prods from within aren't something to ignore. They're your gut, your intuition – your life's most critical data stream, and you're finally listening.

This is a significant moment. Because in doing this work, you've begun to realise something deep – you created that old narrative because your younger, vulnerable self was alone. She didn't have the support she needed through difficult times. But now, you do. You've gained a new appreciation for those parts of you that were kept hidden.

All this tough, gritty work has sparked a new fire within you – a desire to connect with what truly matters now. You're finally starting to understand what I've been saying all along: healing isn't some mythical, woo-woo idea. It's achievable. That's when you lean in and love those hidden parts of yourself. Life doesn't have to be so damn hard all the time. And as for making change, you are beginning to feel that it is possible.

> "What matters most is how well you walk through the fire."
> — Charles Bukowski

Maybe, just maybe, you're beginning to believe me. That experiencing genuine peace and feeling a raw, honest kind of happiness from deep within yourself really can happen. Every. Single. Day.

The Journey So Far

Remember when we first talked about identifying your core values in Book One: *Project Clarity*? About untangling that knotty relationship with food and drink, not through restriction, but by understanding the "why" behind your choices?

And then, in Book Two: *A New Perspective* – well, you were so courageous. You started to really look at your emotional landscape, didn't you? You began to trace the lines of your own emotional blueprint, developing a new perspective on how those past experiences shaped the way you react today. We delved into those triggers, those moments when life felt like a minefield, and we started to learn how to quieten the noise of anxiety with grounding techniques, those little anchors in the storm.

Well, here's the exciting news right from the start – healing makes processing happen faster. It's like you've been wading through thick mud, and now, with the know-how and self-awareness you've cultivated, the ground beneath your feet is becoming firmer, more supportive. Emotions aren't scary monsters anymore; they're your learned friends – your messengers to bring you back, to realign yourself, and to stand up and be responsible for the beautiful woman you are today.

Making Friends with Your Feelings

Think about it. Remember those times when a wave of emotion would hit you – maybe sadness, anger, or fear – and it would feel like being tossed around in a stormy sea? You might have instinctively reached for something to numb the feeling, to distract yourself, or you just tried to bulldoze your way through, pretending everything was fine. And what happened? That unacknowledged visitor just lingered, didn't it? It probably even grew stronger, popping up in unexpected ways, colouring your decisions and draining your energy.

But now? Now you're learning a different way. When an emotion arises, you're becoming skilled at turning towards it with open curiosity. You observe it, like a scientist studying a fascinating specimen. You name it – "Ah, hello, sadness. I see you." You fact-check it. Is this feeling a signal of actual danger, something that requires immediate action to protect yourself? Or is it perhaps communicating something deeper – a whisper from your past, a need that isn't being met?

And here's the magic – when you make room for these feelings, when you allow them to simply be, without judgement or resistance, they don't have to knock you around anymore. They can come into your life, deliver their message, and then, naturally, they begin to move on. You navigate that current challenge with a newfound sense of presence. And the result? You glide. Okay, you may still stumble at times, but you keep on, keeping on. It's not about the challenge disappearing, but about your ability to move through it with so much more ease and speed than before.

The Beautiful, Messy Reality

Now, let's be real. This isn't always a walk in the park. There will be times when facing those deeper emotions feels utterly exhausting. You might feel wiped out, a little lacklustre, like you've run a marathon of the soul. And that's okay. It's a sign that you're doing the work, that you're engaging with yourself on a deeper level. But even in those moments of fatigue, you'll notice that you're still moving forward, perhaps a little slower, but with more grace than when you were caught in the cycle of avoidance.

And let's also be clear – there are no quick fixes in life, are there? Anyone who claims otherwise might be selling you something that simply doesn't exist. Believing you can bypass the complexities of your own heart and history with a magic pill or a fleeting distraction is, well, a form of emotional immaturity – a way of avoiding the beautiful, messy reality of being human.

But when you commit to practising being present, making room for your emotions, and dare I say, making friends with them, you uncover an incredible truth – you can handle life's inevitable ups and downs with much more resilience. Because, guess what, you're showing up and taking responsibility for your emotional health.

> **"Once your mindset changes, everything on the outside will change along with it."**
> – Steve Maraboli

Reflect on the fear that once held you, that constant hum of anxiety that seemed to colour everything. As you heal and learn to trust your ability to navigate your inner world, that fear begins to loosen its grip. And what happens when fear takes a backseat? The world opens up in a new way. It feels … more peaceful. You're not constantly bracing for impact or always on high alert. With that newfound peace comes something valuable – more time to spend on the things that truly bring you joy.

The benefit of consciously choosing to heal those past trauma narratives is vast, my friend. It ripples through every aspect of your life. It's incredibly liberating.

Being able to simply sit with your emotions, to witness them without needing to fix or run from them, is a liberation many people will never experience. It's like finally finding the key to a door you didn't even know was locked. And if you're reading this, if you've come this far, then you have that key. How incredibly lucky are you to possess this skill, this profound ability to be present with yourself?

So, I want to commend you. Commend you for your commitment to your Future Self – that wise and whole woman you are becoming. Thank you for staying the course, for being brave enough to look within.

Now, here we are in Book Three: *Liberated Connection*. In this final book, we're going to build on everything you've learned. For me, this is where all the good stuff happens – saving the best 'til last, you know? Oh, believe me, you still have some work to do, sister, but the load is most definitely lighter. I'll be expecting to see some happy faces at the end of this book, as your glorious energy shines through.

Your Change Experience journey continues, and trust me, the pages where you learn to wholly own your life are still to come.

II.
The Book Structure

A Quick Revisit
A Reminder of the Book's Structure

Just a little reminder, in case it has been a while between reading each book, that each chapter of this book is set up in three neat little sections. Think of it as your own personal GPS for this journey.

🔍 **Education:** First, we'll dive into a topic, so you have all the information you need to get your head around it.

🔗 **Strategy:** Next, we'll get practical with some tools and skills you can use to navigate the choppy waters of life, whether that's to adjust, prepare, or just find a bit of calm.

❓ **Questions/Reflection:** Lastly, you'll find some questions to help you dig deeper and personalise everything you've learned.

The Power of the Questions and Reflections

Alright, let's have another chat about these questions. By now, you're becoming a seasoned pro at this. You've answered a heck of a lot of them over the last two books, and you know they're not just a little quiz at the end of the chapter. They're your personal invitation to dive deeper into what's happening beneath the surface. This is your own coaching time to delve into what's important to you, what's led you here, and the reasons you might be considering change.

This is where you grab that crowbar I mentioned and really get to work. It's your time to prise open the doorway to your inner world and let it all come out – freely, honestly, and with an exemplary old-fashioned commitment to becoming a wholly liberated woman.

You just need to believe you can, permit yourself to take your time, and allow the answers to surface when they're ready. Don't worry if nothing profound appears right away. The answers often reveal themselves in layers, so just sit with the feelings the questions stir up and trust that the messages will emerge in their own sweet time.

> "All truths are easy to understand once they are discovered; the point is to discover them."
> – Galileo Galilei

Your Journal: Your Secret Weapon

Right then, time for another gentle nudge – make sure you have your favourite journal ready! This is your safe space and a trusted companion for your most intimate thoughts.

As always, I'll be inviting you to write down your thoughts, feelings, and answers to the questions. This helps you to connect with your past deeply, figure out what changes you want to make, and keep your vision of your Future Self right in front of you.

And here's a cheeky little tip – once you've written something down, try reading it out loud. Hearing your own voice speak the words is a powerful way to rewire those old narratives in your brain and build a stronger foundation within yourself.

Your Future Self: A Compass for Your Journey

Now that you've done all that magnificent work and have a fantastic new set of skills to look at life differently, I have given you the Future Self Exercise in the appendix to help you revisit and get in touch with the vision of what your future looks like with even greater clarity.

This is something that only you can decide and create. Your Future Self isn't some distant fantasy; she is the roadmap to where you're going. She is the woman you envision becoming – an influential mentor who can help you navigate challenges, face your fears, and find the motivation to make lasting changes.

The idea here is simple but profound. By getting really clear on who you want to be, you can begin to make the small, intentional steps to get there. It's an exercise in moving from a 'victim state' – the "Why does this always happen to me?" mentality – to being an empowered woman. This is about creating a new narrative for yourself, one that isn't defined by past trauma but is built on your new values and a clear vision of the future.

We did a version of this earlier in the series, but now you have more experience and deeper personal insights. By looking at her characteristics, successes, and even her failures, you can build an influential inner advisor. She will be the one who inspires you to act and gives you the freedom to move on from where you are today.

> **"Above all, be the heroine of your life, not the victim."**
> – Nora Ephron

When you revisit the Future Self Exercise in the appendix, take your time with it. You might even find it helpful to draw it out like a mind map, as I did, to get a clear visual of the bigger picture.

> Remember, the person you envision becoming is more influential to you than anyone else. She is your ultimate source of inspiration. Remember, she is your mentor, and she's encouraging you to keep showing up every step of the way.

Let's Begin

1. The Home Stretch

To Become a Liberated Woman
In Touch with Your Genuine Needs

It brings me genuine joy that you've picked up the third book in The Change Experience series. *Liberated Connection* is the final set of building blocks for you to get in touch with your genuine needs and be courageous in your journey of change. All these skills you're building in each chapter will allow you to choose your own path, attract what's truly meant for you, and freely explore the powerful depths of your unique journey as a woman connecting to who you are today.

    This is my favourite part of all this work, what I'm most passionate about, because it's about connecting to and harnessing your innate feminine energy – your birthright. As you've come to know through our time together, I've navigated my share of challenging life experiences. I fundamentally believe these very experiences led me to a radical discovery of my own primal energy, ultimately transforming me into the liberated and very connected woman I am today. In some ways, I see this part of your "self-help evolution" as being the icing on the cake.

    This book is my way of sharing what I've learned; it's me paying it forward and offering a lifeline to the woman within you who is ready – sincerely ready – to reclaim her peace, experience joy, and become deeply comfortable in her authentic self.

After all the work you have already done, these are more building blocks, helping you to go deeper, acquire awareness, and forge an unbreakable connection with all parts of yourself – your beautiful self, trauma, shame, mistakes, the light and dark in it all.

In this new *Liberated Connection* is where you let go. Leaving the past behind you. Metaphorically shedding the skin of visible scars, as you are no longer a victim. You are choosing how you are showing up in the world. For now, you connect to the deep root of trust growing within. Confident in your choices. Loving yourself first. Secure in mutually respectful relationships.

> **"If you do not heal the wounds of your childhood, you will bleed into the future and wound those whom you love."**
> – Unknown

Your Energy and the Art of Connection

Now it's time to explore the very real ways that past experiences can influence your daily life and impact your energy.

If you're sceptical about personal energy, or if you find the term "woo-woo" a bit off-putting, I simply ask you to keep an open mind as you read. I'm going to step it out for you in an easy flow so you can appreciate what it is and why it's essential. Be open, see how the words resonate, and don't make judgements right off the bat, okay?

I want to approach what it means to be hypervigilant, what I sometimes call the "gift from trauma". It is a constant state of being on guard that can drain your energy, affecting everything from your emotional balance and your choices, especially with your automatic quick fixes or tricky relationship with food and/or drink. Whatever it is, it's just another element to be aware of so you can come back to making conscious choices that align with your values.

Then, we'll shift focus to your personal vibration – what raises it, what lowers it, and those "negative energy" moments we all experience. A lot of this you may already know, but you might not appreciate its importance until you see it laid out in the context of our work together.

Next, we arrive at a point in this book where all the pieces come together beautifully. We explore the complementary forces that genuinely shape your inner world – the Feminine (Yin) and the Masculine (Yang) – which, importantly, are not related to your gender. We'll look into how past trauma pushed your mind to develop exhausting survival behaviours for protection, leading you into phases of protection or avoidance. True freedom, you'll discover, doesn't come from fighting these wounded parts; it comes from accepting them. This profound realisation helps you finally feel the pure beauty of feminine energy – intuition, flow, and quiet confidence – that you need to fully embrace the self-trust you deserve today.

We'll learn to recognise "energy vampires" – people who (often unintentionally) leave you feeling drained. More importantly, we'll understand why you might be drawn to these dynamics, especially if you've had challenging relationships in the past. This awareness is the first step in choosing healthier connections. Moving on, you will appreciate that a key part of becoming unstuck is establishing healthy energy boundaries. We'll explore why these boundaries are non-negotiable for maintaining your much-loved peace and joy.

When you are feeling connected, safe within your boundaries, and good about yourself again, it's time to take things a step further. I'll hold your hand as we define a roadmap for creating the life you truly desire. We'll explore strategies to get what you want, introducing a fresh, playful, and energetic adaptation of the S.M.A.R.T. goal-setting technique.

> If you have not heard of the S.M.A.R.T. technique, it is commonly used in coaching to help guide goal setting. S.M.A.R.T. is an acronym that stands for *Specific, Measurable, Achievable, Realistic, and Timely*.

Your Toolkit for Liberation 2.0

Understanding all of the above is only half the story. I have offered six new skills and techniques to add to our Liberation Toolbox, to build on your momentum for making change and living the life you truly want. This book is packed with enlightening and empowering content to lighten the load, so to speak. We'll explore forest bathing (Shinrin-Yoku), drawing on Japanese wisdom to connect with nature's energy for healing. You will learn daily energy practices and my little techniques to help you maintain a higher vibration. You'll discover practical strategies for cultivating and protecting your energy, and learn new grounding techniques using breathwork, movement, and music to anchor you in the present.

There's a dedicated section for energy reflection, offering a guided experience with evocative questions to approach with compassion. You'll be encouraged to acknowledge your past experiences and how they might be manifesting in your repetitive cycles and automatic behaviours in any part of your life. You'll recognise your inner strength and learn to navigate complex emotions with your new grounding tools. This connection to your inner voice will fuel your motivation for positive change.

As you progress, you'll take a moment to acknowledge the remarkable work you've already done. We'll focus on your current priorities and paint a clear picture of your Future Self – exploring what life will feel like as you actively live your values and nurture the energy you deserve. You'll learn to recognise old patterns and consciously choose new, empowering responses.

"You have within you right now, everything you need to deal with whatever the world can throw at you."
– Brian Tracy

Finally, the book concludes with an insightful set of questions about your Change Experience journey, celebrating your progress and solidifying your commitment to your ongoing evolution.

This epic conclusion to the three-part series is a testament to what healed me, and many others like me – and you too (if you allow it). The choice is now yours: turn the page and be inspired to make a deeper connection within – this is your time to take hold of your feminine energy and the power it holds to help you thrive.

My Friend, when I talk about energy, I'm not referring to the energy to get up and walk around the room. I mean the vibration and frequency that everything is made of, from the tiniest shell, the tallest tree, the people you know, to the planets in our vast universe. You, me, every woman reading this – we are all connected – energetically.

A Note

A sidebar between us girls

Here I am, banging this drum again, but it needs to be said – none of what I've shared is rubbish. It's all very doable, but you must put in the effort. I hope, through all these pages, we're aligned on this – your healing is a journey, and please believe me when I say it is so worth it.

You, my friend, have the power to let go of your past so you can step into a future filled with the genuine power you're about to claim. And as I've mentioned before, you need to feel safe while doing this; otherwise, none of it will last. And remember ... your safety is reliant on your choices.

There are no shortcuts here, no pills that will make this easier. You just need to show up, do the work, and trust yourself along the way. That, plus a good dose of bravery, authenticity, compassion, empathy, and acceptance is what you need to heal your most protected core wounds genuinely. Got it?

It's all with you now. And, as you will eventually learn when you back yourself, without a doubt, you will feel a sense of peace that comes from deep within. The kind of joy that isn't just a fleeting high but a quiet, steady truth.

So, put your big girl pants on again, please, and look up. Straighten your posture – no slumping, shoulders back, back straight, hips aligned. Stand tall in your body, and do it for yourself. Yeah. Pay attention to your body as you do this work. She is your best friend. You need her help to get you to the finish line, right? So, listen to her.

> Welcome to your journey of becoming wholly liberated through connection to your truest, most energetic self.

2.
Change Is Not Always Easy

The Hard Truth
Making Changes Can Really Suck Sometimes

Ah, okay, time for some salts of truth here, my friend. I want to talk about the realistic picture of how change can be a little rough at times, and why that is. There is no point creating an illusion that this Change Experience and letting go of the struggle within your Former Self is all roses and rainbows; that's just BS (untrue). So, while I'm holding your hand, and before we get involved in all the great empowering stuff that will follow, can we talk about this for a while?

You know that feeling, right, the knot in your stomach, the catch in your throat – it's an inner fear of letting go. Even when your mind is crystal clear, even when you know moving forward is the only way to bloom, why does it feel like wading through lava sometimes? You're not alone in that struggle, not by a long shot.

You see, there's this fascinating dance happening inside us. Our brilliant frontal cortex, the logical part of our brain, gets it. It sees the sense, the growth, the brighter horizon. "Yes," it says, "let's release what no longer serves us!" But then our limbic brain chimes in, that emotional core, and it's clinging on for dear life. That old narrative, the one we created way back when, especially in those early years. Our limbic brain has a deep, visceral attachment to it. It was our survival manual for so long, wired with a whole history of emotional memories. It feels safe, even if it was ultimately painful.

That's why all this incredible work we're doing – rewiring those old stories, practising our shiny new skills, building this deep inner connection – is not just mental gymnastics. It's about speaking a new language to that emotional centre of your brain, showing it, through consistent action and feeling, that there are new, safer, and more joyful narratives to connect to.

> "And the day came when the risk to remain tight in a bud was more painful than the risk it took to blossom."
>
> — Anaïs Nin

And, oh, I need to be honest here too, whilst I bang on about boundary setting as a must-have life skill, the process isn't always a fun one. It can be an emotional rollercoaster at times too. You start to define your space, to say, "Hey, my needs matter too," and sometimes … people really don't like it. You've played a certain role in their lives, even if it was enabling or handling their less-than-lovely behaviour. When you shift, it throws their equilibrium off, and they might push back, hard. It's just like changing those ingrained food or drink habits (that I talked about in Book One: *Project Clarity*) – resistance is inevitable. You might even hear those hurtful gaslighting labels thrown your way, the accusations designed to make you doubt yourself. And when you stop reliably being that people-pleaser? Suddenly, the dynamic shifts, and conflict can bubble up. Sometimes, you'll choose to step away, and sometimes, those relationships will naturally fade. It can feel … lonely.

This journey of change, this stepping into the unknown – it can trigger that primal fear of being disconnected from your tribe (a potential threat to your survival). Relationships shift, sometimes even disappear, and in those vulnerable moments, that little voice of doubt creeps in. "Am I doing the right thing?" it whispers. And the temptation to run back to the familiar, even if it was unhealthy, can be incredibly strong. That loneliness, that feeling of being challenged in your newfound beliefs, can make it bloody hard to stand your ground. It can make you feel exposed, so you might reach for those old numbing agents – food, alcohol, distractions – just to escape the discomfort. You might even start questioning whether all this hard work is worth the ache. That pull back to the familiar can feel like a magnetic force.

> What you need to release will feel uncomfortable in the moment, but it's the only way to get to the good stuff. The discomfort is temporary; the freedom you'll find is for life.

So, please, be so incredibly gentle with yourself. This isn't an overnight transformation. Unwiring those old narratives, those deep-seated beliefs, that trauma that's been a part of your story for so long – it takes time. And yes, it may take a lot of time. You can't rush healing your core wounds. You've built a strong bond with what lives inside you and untangling that takes patience and a bucket load of kindness. There will be days when you just can't show up for this work with full force, and that's okay.

Patience here means giving yourself months, even a year or more – this is often a lifelong unfolding – to move from that fear-based reaction to change, to a place of genuine confidence in your choices. Letting go is a gradual process of moving through each layer of the unknown, without getting stuck in fear and feeling unsafe.

The beautiful news is, with all this conscious effort, with all your work to create this inner connection, your limbic brain does eventually catch up. As you start to form new healthy attachments (and start letting go of old unhealthy ones), your limbic brain, too, starts to form new attachments, new emotional memories. By taking things one step at a time, one issue at a time, you can do this. Slowly, piece by piece.

If you're tackling boundary setting with those energy vampires (people that suck your energy dry), remember to tackle it one person, one boundary at a time. Trying to do a "scorched earth" clear-out often comes from overwhelming fear and can feel too chaotic in the long run. Go gently, little by little.

So, be kind to yourself through this challenging dance of change. Create space for acceptance. This is about gently releasing those unhealthy attachments and slowly nurturing healthy ones, rooted in the authentic belief that you can let go, you can create new stories,

> **"Growth is painful. Change is painful. But nothing is as painful as staying stuck somewhere you don't belong."**
> – Mandy Hale

you can live safely within your boundaries, and you can experience more positive joy.

What I simply want for you is to see how connecting with your own luminous energy, leaning into that high vibration that resonates with your true self, can help you navigate this discomfort with more gentleness. Because this short-term pain? It's a pathway to a life so much richer than just surviving in that long-term ache.

> And you know what? When you finally stand tall and say, even if quietly to yourself, "My needs matter just as much as yours," you'll do it with a quiet confidence, a deep knowing that you are making choices that simply honour the incredible woman you are.

3. My Trauma Experience

Stockholm Syndrome
The Cycle of Mental and Physical Abuse

In sharing my story, I lay bare a truth that, for so long, felt impossible to even talk about with my friends. What you are about to read is a harrowing account of intense and relentless abuse.

My experience of trauma extended far beyond what any human being should encounter in a home environment. It wove itself into the very fabric of my days through relentless cycles of physical and mental abuse. I was a target for sudden, jarring attacks that left me feeling utterly destabilised – undermined, humiliated, manipulated, and sometimes, physically harmed. I was beaten, held down, and spat upon. Sure, there were days of light and laughter, but then, there would be an air around me thick with ridicule, shame, gaslighting, and cruel mockery.

Within the environment I grew up in, these incidents weren't isolated; they were a pattern, a chilling rhythm of adoration swiftly followed by a sudden, sharp king-hit, a blow both physical and deeply metaphorical, that would send me reeling. Just as quickly, the pendulum would swing back. I would be lifted again, told everything was alright, cherished and included in the mundane normalcy of life as if the storm had never raged.

Growing up, until the fragile years of my adolescence, I learned to navigate this turbulent landscape by retreating inward. As the youngest in my surroundings, I cultivated a vivacious inner world, a safe bubble where I could lose myself in solitary play, undisturbed. My invisible friend and I would stage elaborate shows with my dolls and toys. In my world, the sun shone brightly ... until it didn't.

Tick, tick, tick ... boom. It was like clockwork. I lived with an unsettling knowledge that the periods of calm could be shattered, without warning, at any moment.

Another insidious form this strife took was the casual descent of playful games into something savage. Roughhousing, which wasn't all that joyous or free from pain, was normalised and felt like a passive-aggressive punishment. It was our family's unique brand of fun, conditioning me to believe that things were okay, even when they felt deeply wrong. Play along or else. I became the unwilling recipient of physical battering, torment, ridicule, and soul-crushing shaming. Apparently, it's what I deserved.

Sometimes, it felt like pure, unadulterated hatred directed at me, and the feeling of being unsafe would chill me to my core. Other times, it was masked as playful fighting, laced with jokes and what seemed like friendly laughter, leaving me utterly confused and my young body perpetually tense with unspoken dread. Everything was presented as a joke, a twisted game I had to play along with – or face the consequences. Any flicker of objection on my part would ignite a chain reaction, escalating the playfulness into something forceful and terrifying. Like, like a massive, forceful wave of explosive aggression would be laid on to me, with no protection, or anyone there to stop the attacks. The tears that inevitably followed were met with disapproval, criticism, and the stinging label of "cry-baby" or "drama queen". Then, poof, as if a switch had flipped, the next day I would be adored, as if nothing had ever happened. It was emotional whiplash, again and again and again.

> **"The most common way people give up their power is by thinking they don't have any."**
> – Alice Walker

Build me up, tear me down. Each attack was normalised, minimised, twisted to become my fault for "upsetting things". I had no voice, no way to object to the distorted reality they presented. I learned to cower, to fawn, to become submissive, so desperately reliant on those moments of being built back up that I began to blame myself for the attacks, even when they seemed to erupt from nowhere. It was a bewildering, isolating existence.

When the pain became too much, when I dared to complain, to cry out for help, to beg for it to stop, I was met with gaslighting tactics, deflection, devoid of warmth or empathy. I was told I was making things up, that it didn't happen that way, or that it never happened at all. "You have such a vivid imagination," they'd say with a dismissive wave. Or, "You're just being a drama queen," conveniently shifting the blame onto my tender heart.

My pleas for help vanished into a void of indifference. As an adult, I can now ask the question, "How could those meant to care for me show such a profound lack of concern for my well-being?". As a kid, this is just how things were. It wouldn't be until years later that I began to connect the devastating dots, to understand the motivation behind the gaslighting and the passive creation of these harmful situations. And I wouldn't come to really understand until I had years of therapy that these people were all complicit, and colluded with one another in this environmental toxic zone we lived in. The trauma my caretakers themselves had endured, their own pain and suffering, their cycles of abuse, was generational trauma at its finest. Their experiences meant these types of abusive encounters were normalised within our household.

In my late thirties, a desperate need for answers took hold. Why had the truth been buried? Why was I left to navigate the enduring wreckage of being raped at fifteen, utterly alone, or cast out to deal with a chronic food disorder, like bulimia, on my own? I turned to my main caregiver, the one who knew what had happened, pleading for some understanding of why support vanished, why the lifeline of a psychologist was severed after a mere two visits. The response I received was delivered with a chilling absence of compassion: "If I could get through it, so could you." It was then that I understood. What had happened to me had also happened to her. Robbed of an empathetic witness, abandoned to her own silent suffering, she unknowingly inflicted the same isolation upon me.

Voiceless, I suffered in a suffocating silence. There was no empathetic witness to validate my pain, no one to step in and shield me from the storm. We were all bound together by a toxic shame, a web of pain, loneliness, mistrust, constant abuse, and insidious mental manipulation. What a distorted, terrifying view of the world for a young girl to inherit.

As I explained to you before, on the the outside, I constructed a carefully crafted facade – a persona that was bright, larger than life. Give me a microphone, and you'd have to pry it from my hands. Singing tunes to entertain, I was the life and soul of a party. But behind the closed doors of our family life, the reality was starkly different. There was a ritualistic scapegoating, where I was shamed, degraded, and made to feel infinitely small. It chipped away at my confidence, leaving me constantly waiting, breath held, for the next crumb of praise or acceptance they might toss my way.

Those fleeting moments of "fun" became my only escape, a temporary reprieve from a turbulent reality. When things were good, they were intoxicatingly so. They had a remarkable ability to shower me with attention, to inflate my self-worth, leaving me feeling on top of the world. This intense dependence, a craving so strong that I would brace myself for the inevitable crash, led me to endure the descent into abuse. My subconscious, I believe now, clung to the knowledge that another wave of positive treatment would eventually follow. Heartbreakingly, this became my truth, my twisted mechanism for survival. I rationalised and excused their behaviour, lived in constant fear of them, and yet, in a deeply conflicted and fractured way, I loved them all intensely. My mind held onto the fantasy of the perfect family, and ultimately, the notion that somehow this was all my fault.

For years, this agonising cycle played out. I was kicked, pinned down, spat on, pushed up against a wall in a blanket and repeatedly hit. My hair was pulled, sometimes even ripped out. I was whipped across the face with rough, wet face washers, feeling like leather against my skin as I slept – a cruel punishment for wetting the bed. In front of a crowd, I was pushed into steaming-hot cow manure for the amusement of others. I was made to stand in a paddock while horses were released in a terrifying stampede, leaving me injured and terrified.

At twelve years old, I was even taken to a remote farm with my best friend, a pretty and rather developed girl of thirteen, who all the boys fancied. I was locked in a room and forced to listen to the horrific sounds of her being taken by five drunk teenagers. Against her will. For what happened, I was scolded and shamed, leaving me feeling worthless and unable to trust my own reality. My friend was labelled a slut, expelled from school, and blamed for the whole torrid encounter.

Were any of those boys, one of my family members included, reprimanded for what they did? Not one of them.

> **Please know: The raw reality I describe** – the physical cruelty, the emotional whiplash, the terrifying stampede, and the horrific event at the farm – is an immense burden to carry. It's a truth that should have been acknowledged and protected, not silenced, or twisted. The lack of accountability from those who caused such harm, and the subsequent shaming and blame my friend and I endured, is an act of deep injustice. My statement, "Not one of them was held accountable?" captures the heartbreaking void where empathy and responsibility should have been.
>
> This is a powerful and necessary part of my story. This is where I have had to do a tremendous amount of work on healing my internal narratives and going back to sit with my Inner Child and heal her pain. It speaks volumes about the incredible strength that doing this work possesses to have survived these cycles of cruelty and be here telling you all of this. Let's carry on.

The Next Level of Control

If I spoke up, if I shone too bright, I was clipped down. If a challenge was made to the behaviour, it escalated into abuse, rage, loud voices, and threatening language. And when I learned how to hang up, move away or simply say, "I am not speaking to you when you are like this," the manic behaviour became darker. My life was threatened if I dared to continue to object. The chilling words, "I will hunt you down and chop you up into little pieces," were ringing in my ears. Even these terrifying threats were normalised, and my heart-pounding fear was dismissed, invalidated. And so, I would invite them back into my life, saying, "If you do this again, I will leave, I will cut you off." But you see, I had said that before.

> "You may not control all the events that happen to you, but you can decide not to be reduced by them."
> – Maya Angelou

The physical violence only ceased when I finally created distance, when I no longer lived under the same roof as these individuals. Distance became my reluctant friend, yet the mental abuse persisted. I was tormented for the most insignificant things, constantly put down. I was blamed for circumstances entirely beyond my control, for the family's disappointments. I even began to shame myself for daring to step out, to try to build a life for myself. Every small mistake I made was magnified into a monumental flaw, a defect in my very being. I was forced to swallow fierce statements of my supposed embarrassment to the family, my inherent unworthiness, all in a desperate attempt to remain within the fragile orbit of the family unit. Whatever I did – in the public arena of our family rhetoric – I was deemed a failure, all packaged up in a dismissive joke, a cutting remark meant to toughen me up, to tell me to "drink a cup of cement". Alcohol was my dear friend and my saviour from the reality of this confusing and shameful existence.

I lived this way until my early forties, feeling mentally frayed and deeply insecure. It was then that I sought the help of a psychotherapist who gently, yet firmly, explained to me that I was a victim of abuse. I remember the shock, the utter inability to even utter the word "abuse". I couldn't bring myself to criticise or blame these people. I loved them; how could this be abuse? "These people are my best friends," I told my therapist, desperately trying to characterise our deeply fractured relationships.

My "aha" moment came with the understanding that in a family of origin, everyone unconsciously plays a role. Suddenly, the chaotic pieces began to fall into place, and I started to see the insidious patterns that had defined my life. My therapist guided me in how to disengage from the role I had been forced to play within that unit. Gosh, it was a tumultuous, painful process.

The anxiety attacks, the gnawing fear, the resentment that began to simmer and then boil – it was overwhelming. And all the while, the cycles continued, and I, in my ingrained patterns, kept showing up. Dramatic scenarios would unfold, seemingly designed to pull me back into the fold under the guise of being "needed". Then, as I grew wiser and tentatively began to set boundaries against this toxic, symbiotic link of shame, the attacks would escalate in severity. I learned to recognise the signs, sometimes managing to sidestep them, often failing.

Breaking free from such a deeply entrenched symbiotic relationship is a complex, agonisingly sticky process that rarely ends smoothly for anyone involved. Ideally, kindness and compassion would pave the way, but when one party attempts to sever the connection, it often devolves into a cruel and brutal struggle. In my case, the ending was catastrophic. There was one final attack I couldn't evade, though I must confess, I played a role in provoking it. Years of suppressed rage finally found its voice in a torrent of colourful words.

Demonic fights can never be won alone, and I lost, undeniably. It was a terrifying scene, worthy of a dark Netflix script, leaving me with devastating emotional wounds and a permanent severing of ties. Yet, as some say, everything happens for a reason, at the right time. As excruciating as it was, there's a twisted sense in which the pain and the profound isolation that followed were worth it, if it meant it was the last attack I would ever endure from them. (As I have alluded to previously, this is where the necessity of requiring my hip replacement was born.)

If you know or understand Stockholm syndrome, then you have a framework for comprehending what I endured, what I suffered. That was my reality. I loved the people I grew up with – yes, even the ones who inflicted such deep wounds. The volatile swings from kindness to terror, the insidious behaviours of gaslighting, manipulation, and scapegoating – it was all I knew, all that felt "normal". I was trapped in these cycles, seemingly without escape, clinging to a desperate fantasy of an ideal, loving, and supportive family life. I protected them, defended them, yearned to love them with my whole heart. I would even become their cheerleader, enthusiastically telling my friends how wonderful they were.

It took an immense amount of therapy to finally grasp the truth: What happened to me was abuse. The word itself felt foreign, impossible to utter. The chasm between the idealised vision in my head and the harsh reality of my existence dumbfounded me. It was an incredibly lonely and disorienting time, I can assure you.

Now, I accept it. Now, I see it clearly for what it was, and it fuels my passion – though even that word feels inadequate – to speak openly about abuse. Because I believe more people need the strength and the confidence to break the silence. We need to normalise the painful truth that this happens within families, within the very places that are supposed to be our safest havens.

I have come to understand that with the light, there is always the dark. And to sever the deep roots of that symbiotic attachment, I had to make a conscious, difficult choice – a choice to find my own peace. I knew I couldn't win, couldn't plead my case to be heard by those who were determined to keep me in the role they had assigned me. My words would only be ridiculed, slammed back in my face. Disconnection, complete severance of communication, became my only path to that elusive peace. And, I must say, it brought the quiet I so desperately craved, a freedom from the relentless storms and tornadoes that had defined those relationships, from those soul-destroying moments of being king hit out of nowhere, on days when I dared to believe the sun was shining.

The other side of this hard-won peace, however, brings its own kind of ache. On days like Christmas and the Easter long weekend, a deep melancholy can wash over me, like an intense sadness. I miss the people my Inner Child loved so much. I hold on to the memories of laughter, fun, and happy times that weren't laced with a personal attack aimed at me. It's a significant trade-off, you see, slightly bordering on maintaining a fantasy of family should be like. And so, I consciously choose to allow myself to feel the pain, the sadness, the loneliness that bubbles up on these commercially branded, "must-be-happy-family days". I create space for those emotions to flow in, and just as importantly, to flow back out again.

Now, I tend to spend these significant holidays alone, surrounded by my beloved fur babies. To force myself into social situations would mean suppressing the very real emotions churning within me, putting on a false happy face for the sake of others. That simply doesn't work for me anymore. Instead, I choose to honour my feelings, to listen to the messages of my inner "Fleur-Elizabeth" voice, allowing them all to take form, gently and with deep compassion. And then, with a quiet confidence, I know

I can move on, as I should. Feeling beautifully connected to my Former Self and who I am today. Whole. Authentic. Liberated.

Like me, there are many of you out there who have endured the insidious cycle of abuse. The cuts, bruises, shame, even a broken hip and a smashed face – these physical wounds can heal, though they leave their scars. But the damage this kind of trauma inflicts on our trust, our sense of self, our inner peace – that takes far longer to mend, demanding a sincere and ongoing commitment to healing. This is the work I have done, and I am not ashamed to say that it is a journey I will continue for the rest of my life.

> **"The unhappiest people in this world are those who care the most about what other people think."**
> – C. JoyBell C.

There's an expression, "Envy someone until you reach their front door." Everything may appear perfect on the surface, but you cannot see the hidden realities behind closed doors. This is especially true in families who are masters of keeping up appearances, diligently concealing their toxic secrets of abuse. None of this is pretty, my dear friend, none of it. But in sharing our truths, we begin to dismantle the silence and step into the light.

I recognise this is a deeply moving and powerful account of trauma and survival. Given the themes of hidden abuse, distorted reality, the struggle for self-worth, and the journey to self-acceptance and freedom – it's a lot, I know.

> I wanted to share this to demonstrate that resilience emerges from adversity. More importantly, this resilience is anchored in the quiet strength found through my own emotional and energetic healing.

IMPORTANT NOTE: This brutal cycle of abuse I describe – a chilling rhythm of building up followed by a sharp takedown – is a widespread form of psychological manipulation.

From a clinical perspective, this pattern of intermittent positive and negative reinforcement is a highly effective way for an abuser to establish and sustain power and control. By sporadically offering moments of warmth, validation, and normalcy, the abuser builds a strong trauma bond. This deep, complex attachment leaves the victim (in this case, let's assume it is you) desperately longing for the "good" moments while enduring the abuse.

This emotional rollercoaster, as I called it, amplified by gaslighting that dismisses your reality, systematically damages your self-esteem and ability to trust your own perceptions. You are conditioned to believe the abuse is your fault, leading to learned helplessness and a constant state of hypervigilance, where you live in ongoing fear of the next attack. The abuser's behaviour often stems from their own unhealed trauma, or intergenerational trauma, perpetuating a toxic cycle that leaves you isolated, confused, and dangerously dependent on the very person harming you.

Unpacking
Your Energy

4.
Navigating Your Inner Power

Your Energy, Unpacked
Understanding What Your Energy Means to You

Negative Energy	Positive Energy
Being Isolated	Being Connected
Hiding Behind a Mask	Living Authentically
Automatic Trigger Behaviours	Making the Right Choices
Emotional Disconnection	Living By Your Values
Ignoring Your Gut	Feminine Power Perception, Intuition
Difficulty Communicating	
Seek Validation from Others	Trusting Yourself
	Likeminded People
Energy Vampires	High Vibration
Low Vibration	Trusting Your Gut
Unhealthy Mind and Body	Healthy Mind and Body
	Earth Connection
Reliances on Pharmaceuticals	Self-Awareness
Avoiding Self-Reflection	

Being Connected

To help grasp the concept of creating a deep connection with your personal energy and embarking on this journey, I've broken it down into bite-sized elements for you to read through and take on board. Think of this as education and awareness into the different facets of your inner power. Hopefully, this will give you some real food for thought.

So, What Exactly is Energy?

When I talk about energy, I'm really talking about what I call "being connected." It's far richer than a fleeting positive buzz; it's the very fabric of your life, the backbone of your being. It's the real presence of your precious feminine qualities.

Being connected means turning up the volume on your inner message centre. Your innate nurturing spirit and those insightful, intuitive nudges that guide you – you hear them so much clearer now. This changes everything. The essence of your creativity and that light, open receptivity to life's ebb and flow are now at the forefront, rather than taking a backseat to all the chaos.

It's a potent force that links you to your femininity and inner beauty (no matter how you look in the morning!). When you're connected, tuning into your gut feels effortless, and that big word – transformation – feels so much more within reach.

You'll also notice you start attracting people who are more aligned with your newfound footing in life and your evolving values. And it's how people experience you, too. Do you feel good to be around, or are you a real drag?

Being connected allows you to shift your mindset from scarcity to abundance, especially when you're in any environment where you feel utterly safe, deeply seen, and unconditionally supported.

> **"A woman is the full circle. Within her is the power to create, nurture and transform."**
> – Diane Mariechild

Ultimately, your energy is your unique signature in action – it's the authentic self you project into the world.

🔎 Why is it Important to You?

This incredible "primal feminine power" – as I like to call it – is your birthright. It's a gift to enable you to thrive while you're here on this earth. It's all about a fierce alignment with your authentic self, setting beautiful boundaries, and honouring your core values.

When you're connected to this powerful inner knowing, you have the clarity to define your needs, to make choices that genuinely resonate with who you are, and to stand firm in the confidence of your decisions. This energy supports you through the ups and downs, the highs and lows, and through the tests you're given to ensure you're walking the right path.

Your energy is *you* – your whole self. Think of it as your new friend who always has your back. It's your life's compass, always letting you know where you stand.

How Do You Feel it?

Close your eyes and feel every part of your body. Every inch of you is attuned to your energy, and it's the most powerful communicator, telling you what's truly going on within. It's time to step up and trust that unwavering inner voice – that innate intuition guiding you through life. It's a very real and present gift if you dare to allow yourself to feel it.

Here's a beautiful truth. When you are living in alignment with your authentic self and your values, that pure flow of energy will be in absolute abundance within you. That's you connected to your most authentic self. You can feel it every day, in every place, in any outfit or pair of shoes. It's just a feeling, a connection that only you can grasp.

Remember your Inner Child work from Book Two: *A New Perspective*? Those deep, intense emotions you felt? That's your body's energy communicating. It's a robust inner conversation that connects your current self with the person you used to be.

🔍 Where Do You Find It?

You know that saying, "Stop looking; you've found me"? Well, my friend, that's what you need to say to yourself. Your energy is all within you. Yes, there are ways to connect to it more profoundly, of course, but it's primarily an inside job. It's up to you to reach in and take hold of it.

To help you, simply think of those quiet moments of self-reflection, those intuitive nudges you've learned to trust, the joy that flows when you're creating, and those loving-myself-actions that undoubtedly replenish your soul. You can learn to appreciate the level of your energy in these ways.

People you meet are also conductors of energy. You can easily take on another person's energy, so that's something to be mindful of. It can be a good, positive, and uplifting force, or it can be draining and depleting.

Another beautiful truth is that energy is also all around you. We are all connected by this incredible web. Most magnificently, it comes from the very earth beneath our feet, in the gentle rustling of the trees, and in the same air we breathe. It's a gift that's always accessible.

🔍 What Can it Do for You?

When you are connected, things really start to shift. Honestly, stepping into this space of truly owning your powerful energy is the next level of liberation. It fosters a learned sense of "knowing" and acceptance of yourself, which dissolves the need for negative self-talk. It brings a wonderful sense of balance to your life, and when you have a bad day or stumble, it holds you with compassion and makes room for self-empathy as a gift. Imperfections are allowed without punishment. Remember that.

This connection allows you to filter through the noise of the world so much faster, as your senses become incredibly aware and heightened. It helps you recognise your triggers, or those people who might upset you, with such clarity and speed – without taking all the blame.

As I mentioned before, processing becomes faster, empowering you to make wiser decisions and protect yourself (and your health) from things that once threw you completely off course.

Remember, it's all part of believing in your capacity to make change. Because in this place, even the smallest adjustment to your lens can offer the greatest gifts. A wide-open door to a deeper, non-judgemental understanding of yourself.

> "You are a creature of light. You have the power to draw in all that is good, simply by being who you are."
>
> – Iyanla Vanzant

 ## What's Blocking Your Light?

Oh, my friend, it really breaks my heart to say this, but sometimes so many hurdles stand in the way of us embracing our own radiant energy. We're often caught in a whirlwind of hypervigilance, where our energy can feel like a delicate plant starving for light and water. It just withers, with no chance to thrive.

Then there's that relentless pressure to "keep up" and "measure up" – a real energy killer if you ask me. We get trapped in roles, trying to meet expectations that just don't fit, all while feeling the weight of needing to be accepted. We're still carrying those old, ingrained biases we took on as children, just to feel loved.

And those lingering stories of our past challenges – the trauma we've faced – leave deep imprints. They fuel that cruel inner critic with its whispers of, "I'm not worthy," "I'm not enough," or "I'm not good enough." There's the ambivalence, that strange, uncomfortable/comfortable place of staying stuck. Those sneaky little narratives make us doubt ourselves, whispering, "What if I fail?" So, we stay put, stagnant.

And then, there's that self-imposed pressure to act in a certain way just to fit in, to be liked, even when it feels so utterly wrong. All these things can dim our light, making it harder to embrace our energy and see this Change Experience journey through. These barriers are our own chains, keeping our vibrations low and our ability to propel forward out of our reach.

You feel like a victim, repeating old patterns, unable to take responsibility for yourself, wanting to point fingers at everyone else for the pain. We go backwards, checking into our 24-hour-access motel called "Stays-Stuck." Your Future Self, that beautiful vision you once had, becomes a distant dream. Your vibration may rise from a temporary quick fix, like some tasty sugary treats or feeling fabulous after four glasses of wine, but soon after, it returns to the great depths of depressive lows. You start to see the world through a cloudy lens once again.

The People Who Will Find You

You know, those beautiful souls who are meant to connect, they always find each other. As you journey through your unique Change Experience, some people might naturally drift away, while others will walk right into your life. When you fully step into your authentic energy, you'll naturally draw in those who resonate with your truth.

But those who used to drain you – the "energy vampires," as I call them – they might just be the ones who reject you now. They might feel uncomfortable with your new radiance or even try to dim your light so they can feel bigger.

Take a moment now and picture those faces. See them clearly – look at those who are drawn to your light and those who shrink away.

What Skills Do You Need?

I'm going to share some more energy-affirming skills in this book, don't you worry. But let's chat about this a bit now, so you get a real feel for what it means to deepen your connection to your own energy.

First off, you need to ground yourself, to sink roots into the earth, to call your energy fully into your being and really feel its buoyant presence. Then, there's the beautiful practice of self-reflection, taking ownership of your role in life, just as we explored in Book Two: *A New Perspective*. Taking the reins in piloting your emotions with grace through emotional regulation is a game-changer, and you know how to do that now.

Setting clear intentions is a must-have skill for embracing energy. And, oh, the art of setting clear and healthy boundaries is vital. It's also a must-have, trust me.

Acceptance is another skill you know about. Accept who you are and accept your innate worthiness of being seen and valued as a whole person, not someone who's lost a part of herself because she's suffered. Your value is non-negotiable. Embrace every unique piece of who you are and forgive yourself for the shame and blame you've been carrying. That's the self-empathy you've also got in your back pocket. We all have our light and shadow, and we all hold parts of ourselves captive. It's time to turn the lights back on in those hidden places.

This is your cue to find a connection. There's the skill of living in alignment with your values, taking back control of those automatic behaviours, and becoming the director of your own life. You get to choose your reactions, discern your responses to triggers, and choose your path towards your Future Self, even when it feels a bit uncertain. Learn to trust yourself. Trust that you can show up for yourself, especially when it matters most.

> "The intuitive mind is a sacred gift, and the rational mind is a faithful servant. We have created a society that honours the servant and has forgotten the gift."
> – Albert Einstein

Build those supportive relationships with the beautiful, weird, and wonderful people who get you, who accept you, who lift you up, and who will be there as a source of strength in your corner. And finally, focus your precious energy on the activities and connections that genuinely resonate with what is important to you. What do you really need and desire? What are the things that bring you home-grown peace, joy, and happiness?

What Superpowers Does It Give?

Make no mistake, my friend, when you choose to let go and allow your energy to flow, you are taking hold of a new superpower.

Wouldn't you love to trust yourself implicitly, listening to every message your gut sends you, having crystal-clear intuition and perception? How about feeling proud of living every day of your life, feeling good in your

> **"Everything is energy and that's all there is to it. Match the frequency of the reality you want and you cannot help but get that reality. It can be no other way. This is not philosophy. This is physics."**
> – Darryl Anka (as Bashar)

skin? Imagine being able to communicate your needs rather than denying them, while still caring for everyone else.

Imagine feeling comfortable setting and maintaining healthy boundaries, so you don't feel drained, overwhelmed, or taken for granted by those who haven't set boundaries themselves. Can you imagine being gloriously connected to your creativity, exploring parts of yourself you dreamed of as a child but became too afraid to try as an adult? And stepping into an incredible resilience that is both graceful and fiercely strong – wouldn't that be a treat!

Honestly, connecting to this whole energy thing is your own unique kind of magic! It's all yours; you just have to reach out and grab it.

A Note

A sidebar between us girls

My friend, connecting to your energy isn't some mystical or unattainable thing. In all honesty, none of what I'm sharing in the following lines should be new to you – I'm hoping it's more of a gentle reminder. So, here you go, how about thinking of connecting to and owning your energy like this? It's about:

- Cultivating a new ear to listen.
- Tapping into an awareness of the subtle yet powerful currents that flow within you.
- Taking notice of the subtle shifts happening inside.
- Opening to the new narratives in your head.
- Ending your relationship with the inner critic.
- Being true to yourself, without fuss or chaos.
- Ending the temporary highs and quick fixes (because, let's be honest, they're an instant energy killer the next day).
- And, noticing the expanded know-how, you must make a change within your world.

It all sounds straightforward, right? But I know none of this is a walk in the park. Hence why you're building new skills and a capacity to make change – and now changes in your energetic connection. By nurturing your energy and taking these points above into greater consideration, life truly will get easier. You'll have greater clarity, resilience, and a very real, lovely sense of inner peace.

> As I said, this primal energy is your birthright, and it's waiting for you to trust yourself enough to explore what is there.

5.
Good and Not-So-Good Vibrations

Decoding Energy Connection
A Path to Living Authentically

Have you ever walked into a room and immediately felt the vibe was heavy, or sensed tension, making you uneasy? That's the collective energy of everyone in the room – their thoughts, vibrations, and intentions. It can feel daunting, right? Or have you entered a space where everyone was happy, smiling, and you instantly felt great, smiling back, and feeling buoyant? That, too, is the collective energy of the room, reflecting people's thoughts, vibrations, and intentions. Your returned smile and good feeling – that's you mirroring their energy, meeting their vibrations. Does that make sense?

    Now, have you ever felt a subtle hum beneath the surface of your being? That quiet but distinct feeling, that inner compass gently nudging you in one direction or another? That, my friend, is your energy – a dynamic, powerful force that is uniquely yours. It's a gift with immense potential, if you're willing to "let the genie out of the bottle", so to speak. Learning to connect with it, positively feeling its currents and listening to its whispers can unlock a profound transformation in your life. It can guide you towards balance, joy, and a sense of authenticity you may have only dreamed of – perhaps aligning with the Future Self you identified back in Book One: *Project Clarity*.

Think of your energy as the bedrock of your Future Self. When you're in tune with it, you become acutely aware of what nourishes you and what depletes you. This awareness ripples through every aspect of your existence, starting with the choices you make. When your energy is grounded and clear, you move from reaction to intention. You can discern what simply aligns with your values, what feels authentic and correct for you, rather than being swayed by old patterns, external pressures, or the lingering echoes of past trauma. You begin to make choices that genuinely serve your highest good, paving the way for a deeper, more sustainable happiness.

This grounded energy acts as a powerful anchor, especially when manoeuvring the complexities of relationships. When you're connected to your own energetic field, you become more attuned to the energetic vibrations of others. You can sense who lifts you up, who feels safe and supportive, and conversely, who leaves you feeling drained or uneasy. This intuitive awareness allows you to naturally gravitate towards healthier connections, fostering relationships built on mutual respect and genuine care. You might find yourself gently creating distance from those who consistently deplete your energy, not out of malice but a deep commitment to your own healing Change Experience journey. More on that later.

> **"Your work is to discover your world and then with all your heart give yourself to it."**
> – **Buddha**

The impact on your physical and mental health is equally profound. Being in tune with your energy means being deeply connected to your body's wisdom. You start to notice the subtle cues – a persistent fatigue, a knot in your stomach, a tightness in your chest – not as inconveniences to ignore but as messages from your inner self. This heightened awareness allows you to respond to your body's needs with greater care and intention, potentially reducing stress and anxiety by addressing imbalances before they escalate.

One of the most liberating aspects of connecting to your energy is its ability to help you recognise and move through your triggers with greater ease and speed. When you're grounded, you can feel the subtle shift in your energy that signals an old wound being touched. Instead of being instantly swept away by the emotional storm, you can observe it with a sense of presence. Now, understanding that this is a familiar old narrative ripple effect from the past, not necessarily the reality of the present moment. This awareness creates space for you to respond with more intention and less reactivity, gradually diminishing the power of those triggers and fostering a greater sense of inner balance. The emotional storms that once threatened to capsize your life begin to lose their intensity and frequency.

Following on from the work we've just done in Book Two: *A New Perspective*, this adds another layer to your skill set. You see with clarity that emotions are simply messengers, carrying valuable information about your inner landscape. By allowing them space, without judgement or fear, you begin to regulate them more effectively. You learn that you can feel sadness without being consumed by it, experience anger without acting destructively, and embrace joy with an open heart.

And this, my friend, leads us to the exquisite power of connecting with your feminine energy. This isn't about gender in a limiting sense; it's about embracing the inherent qualities within us all that are often associated with the feminine – intuition, inner voice, softness, vulnerability, nurturing, and very real loving-myself-actions. When you consciously connect to this aspect of your energy, your intuition sharpens, that quiet knowing within becomes a trusted guide. You tap into a deep knowledge centre of skills and discernment that you have never used to your advantage before.

> **"Everything is energy, and that's all there is to it. Match the frequency of the reality you want, and you cannot help but get that reality. It can be no other way. This is not philosophy. This is physics."**
> – Albert Einstein

Embracing your softness allows you to be vulnerable without feeling fragile. You create a space where you can be seen and accepted, both by yourself and by others. Listening to yourself becomes a sacred practice, honouring your needs and desires without guilt or apology. Loving-myself-actions transforms from a luxury to a non-negotiable act of know-how.

This newfound skill of harnessing your feminine energy naturally fosters more meaningful connections in your life. You attract those who resonate with your authentic self, creating a supportive and nurturing circle that genuinely understands and honours your journey.

> You become less concerned with the quantity of people around you and more focused on the quality of your relationships.

Tuning In
How Your Liberation Toolbox Aligns with Your Higher Vibration

Making another reference to Book Two: *A New Perspective*, do you recall one of the final, essential skill-building exercises – your Liberation Toolbox?

These weren't merely concepts relating to and for emotional regulation; I'd like to impress how they are practical, hands-on tools designed to liberate you from being stuck and to amplify your energetic power, enabling you to navigate life's twists and turns with greater ease and grace. As we now explore the intricacies of your energetic vibrations, you'll discover how deeply interconnected they are.

Think of it this way: The tools you've cultivated – embracing your authenticity, offering yourself deep self-empathy, nurturing unwavering self-trust, harnessing the power of breathwork, learning and growing by normalising mistakes, and cultivating sincere acceptance – are all powerful keys to your inner connection, enabling you to unlock and maintain a dynamic, high-frequency energy. They work together to clear away the energetic clutter, allowing your natural light to shine brightly as you move through this powerful Change Experience and step into the embrace of your Future Self.

> **"Freedom is found in the stillness of the heart, where every path is clear and all voices but your own are hushed."**
> – Lao Tzu

Let's start with connecting to your **authenticity**. It's about finding what simply resonates within you. When you honour that inner voice, when your actions and expressions align with your deepest values and feelings, your energetic frequency becomes clear and strong. There's no grating imbalance, no internal conflict creating energetic drag. It's like a pure, unwavering note being played. Stress, denial, and those heavy, negative emotions simply can't take root as easily when you're living in your truth. Your energy flows freely, and you're not burdened with the need to be someone you're not.

> I now believe that the word "authenticity" also means "beautiful woman" in my own world.

Then there's the connection to **self-empathy**, which I believe is tuning into the voice of your own heart, listening to your needs and struggles without judgement. Seeing yourself as a whole being, imperfections, and all, creates a powerful energetic coherence. When you meet your own vulnerabilities with kindness and understanding, you heal those little energetic tears that can lower your vibration. This, also a form of self-acceptance, allows your inner light to shine without obstruction and, in turn, allows others to see and connect with the authentic you. It fosters a sense of wholeness that resonates at a higher frequency.

Now, **trusting yourself** is the most powerful bedrock for your liberation. When you absolutely back yourself, believe in your inner wisdom, in your intuition, then you create an unshakeable energetic foundation. Doubt and second-guessing create energetic instability, but self-trust anchors you in a higher frequency of certainty and confidence. As you navigate this Change Experience, this unwavering belief in yourself will be a guiding light, ensuring you make choices that serve your highest good and the vision of your Future Self.

Now, let's talk about the incredible gift of **practising powerful breathwork**. Remember how you discovered its ability to shift your emotional triggers? Conscious breathing is like an instant energetic reset button. It can move you from a low vibration of stress or anxiety to a higher state of calm, clarity, and presence. By intentionally working with your breath, you're actively tuning your energetic instrument, bringing it into harmonious resonance. You allow yourself to connect more deeply with your intuition and inner guidance as you navigate your immediate needs and those of your Future Self.

Learning and growing by **normalising mistakes** is another vital tool in your connection kit, as you already know. Seeing missteps not as failures but as opportunities for growth is energetically liberating. Holding onto shame or regret creates a heavy, low vibration. But when you approach your experiences with curiosity and a willingness to learn, you transmute that energy into know-how and resilience. This forward-moving energy is essential for shepherding change, becoming connected, and stepping confidently towards your Future Self.

Finally, **acceptance**, my favourite, is like the tonic that soothes and elevates your entire world. When you can meet yourself, others, and the circumstances of your life with a spirit of acceptance, you release the energetic resistance that comes with resentment, judgement, and struggle. This allows your vibration to rise. Think of it like sowing your garden beds to cultivate your own home-grown peace and joy. It's in this state of acceptance that you have a much better chance of connecting with your inner voice, observing yourself, and truly taking note. She, your inner voice, is not being asked to hide away anymore, right?

And, if you haven't been able to work out what your purpose is yet, perhaps in this place, your lens may just shift. You may even start to work out what might bring some genuine meaning to your pursuits. What might give life a different meaning. What small, different way of thinking about that tiny thing that sparked your interest, will truly make a difference.

In this place, you won't struggle with your values so much either, because the narrative changes when you hone the skill of acceptance. Why, because there is much more honesty going on, isn't there? So, ultimately, that means less turbulence, right?

Then, what I'd truly hope for you is that you gracefully start to grab hold of this beautiful place you're creating inside yourself. And trust that taking on the skill of acceptance with a calm and open heart is all part of the plan.

Remember this: Your core self, wrapped up with lots of kindness. Grounded. Full of trust. Deep breathing, eyes open, ears listening. Learning always and accepting what is – that's what makes a clear, strong vibration, right there!

> That's the good stuff that
> lights your way forward.

The Next Level Connection
Tuning In (with a little wiggle!)

Okay, my friend, did you nod at any of the last bits? Yes, okay, so you're feeling okay with this energy stuff, right? Awesome! Because honestly, it's not some woo-woo mystery only for gurus on mountaintops. It's in the everyday stuff, and guess what? You're already doing it! So, let's peek behind the curtain and see how you can crank up the good vibes in your everyday life.

Think of your "vibration" as the unique song you're constantly playing out into the world. You know how, when you hear a killer tune, you can practically *feel* it in your bones? It resonates, right? Well, *you're* that incredible instrument, capable of producing the most exquisite music. When your vibration is high and harmonious, life flows with more ease, joy, and those feel-good connections we all crave. Understanding and consciously nudging that vibration higher? My lovely friend, that's like unlocking your inner Rockstar and turning the volume up on a life that truly sings …

> … even if it's just in the shower each morning!

"You have a treasure within you that is infinitely greater than anything the world can offer."
– Eckhart Tolle

So, how do we get that inner band jamming on a higher key? It's simpler than you think, my friend – it's all about nourishing that magnificent inner instrument of yours with the good stuff. Think of it like giving your soul a spa day and a belly laugh all rolled into one! Sounds good, doesn't it?

You can start to work on these actions today:

🔗 Some good old-fashioned love and compassion (aka the heart fluffers)

Seriously, this is the top-shelf stuff. Cultivating that warm, fuzzy feeling for yourself *and* others (including our fur babies, right?) – that's like hitting the highest, most beautiful notes on the vibrational scale. Think of the capacity to love yourself like a cosy, warm blanket. And empathy, that's like a warm, yummy hug. It creates this amazing upward spiral of good energy. Who knew being loving could be so uniquely powerful?

🔗 It's very simple to show gratitude (and it's kind of like magic!)

My friend, this one's like a secret weapon. Regularly acknowledging all the good stuff in your life, big or tiny – every single day. It's like flipping a switch that shines a spotlight on abundance and positivity. Suddenly, your focus shifts from what's missing to all the amazing things you *do* have, and TING! Your frequency gets a lovely little lift.

For example, I went and thanked the lady who collects my bins each week today; she was chuffed. A thankless task, for sure, but, hey, I'm always grateful. And, the net result, she felt good and so did I. It's like the universe winks and says, "See? Plenty of good stuff here!"

🔗 Joy, joy, and more joy (the little things that are good for your soul!)

Okay, this one's a no-brainer, right? Doing things that bring you genuine, unadulterated joy? That's pure, high-octane vibrational fuel! (But it's very different to the high-octane buzz you probably felt, hitting hard on the sauce (alcohol) or running a million miles an hour on some temporary high!) It doesn't have to be complicated – the simplest pleasures often pack the biggest energetic punch. So go dance in the kitchen, sing in the shower, plant a new dahlia and watch it bloom gorgeous flowers that make your heart sing – whatever tickles your funny bone and lights you up!

∞ A good old' belly laugh (warning: may cause happy tears!)

Seriously, my friend, let yourself loose and have a proper, deep-down belly laugh! Find those things that make you snort with glee. It's like releasing a whole bunch of stagnant energy and letting in this light, expansive feeling. Plus, who doesn't feel amazing after a good laugh? It's like a mini energetic cleanse!

> It's also contagious, have you noticed?
> When you laugh uncontrollably, others
> spontaneously laugh too, for no reason. Why?
> Because we are all connected. That's why!

∞ Kindness and generosity of spirit (sprinkle that goodness around!)

Simple acts of kindness? They create this incredible ripple effect of positive energy, both for you and for others. It's like throwing a pebble into a pond and watching those lovely ripples spread out. It not only feels good to give, but it also sends a clear signal to the universe that you're all about the good stuff, and you attract more of it right back to you.

∞ Good old' mother earth (nature's high-vibe hug!)

Have you ever just stood barefoot on the grass or taken a deep breath in a botanical garden or forest? TING! Instant good vibes. Nature is like this massive, powerful conductor of high-frequency energy. Immersing yourself in its beauty, feeling that earth connection, breathing that fresh air? It's like plugging directly into "the source" and giving your energetic spirit an instant lift. Think of it as a natural energy spa, totally free and utterly amazing. More on this later.

∞ Get creative, sister (let your inner artist loose!)

Energy pours from creative sources. Whether you're fingerpainting like a carefree kid, pouring out your deepest thoughts in a journal, singing with full voice in the shower, or simply dancing like no one is watching, express yourself as if the audience doesn't exist and see what happens. Alternatively, channel your energy into creative activities like gardening, my new passion. The sheer act of nurturing and seeing growth brings an immense release of joy and vibrant energy. Or simply fiddling with something crafty – anything that sparks your unique creative energy is pure gold. It's like discovering the secret recipe for the best home-grown fertiliser to cultivate happiness and joy in your life.

> I dare you to get your wooden spoon, put on a t-shirt, your comfy undies, maybe even a pair of high heels, and sing your heart out. Howl to the moon, sister, and love every note (in key or not!). Go on. Don't be shy. Get your creative joy on!

🔗 Do yourself a favour and be present (ditch the yesterdays and tomorrows!)

You know that mental hamster wheel of worrying about the past or stressing about the future? Yeah, that's a major vibe killer. Bringing your awareness right here, right now, is like dropping anchor in a sea of calm. It instantly elevates your energetic frequency. Showing up fully for the moment? That's a huge act of self-love and a powerful way to keep your energy clear and bright.

🔗 Eating right, what goes in is only the good stuff (you are a bio-individual, remember?)

Think of your body as this incredible, finely tuned machine. What you put in it totally affects how it runs, right? Listening to what *your* unique body thrives on – mostly natural, whole, unprocessed goodness? That's like giving your machine the premium fuel it deserves. These vibrant sources of energy contribute to a higher overall vibration. It's not about being perfect; it's about nourishing your amazing self from the inside out.

🔗 Move your booty (shake off the stagnant stuff!)

Seriously, get your body moving in ways that feel good! Whether it's walking, stretching, or dancing. Anything that gets your circulation going and your heart pumping – it's like shaking off any stagnant energy. You feel energised and alive, and that physical movement totally boosts your overall vibe. Plus, it's super fun!

The Lower Vibes
That We Must Be Aware Of

Now, heads up, my friend! Just like there are things that lift you up, there are things that can **significantly lower your vibration**, creating this yucky dissonance in your inner tune and making life feel ... well, heavy. Let's peek at a couple of the sneaky culprits:

🔗 **Your Former Self's unwanted behaviours (yes, it's time to ditch the old baggage!)**
Those automatic, not-so-helpful patterns of behaviour that don't serve your healing, Change Experience and inner purpose to connect. Whether they're old coping mechanisms or just habits you've outgrown, they can create energetic blockages and seriously dim your overall frequency. It's like having a scratchy record playing in the background of your life. Sister, it is time to gently release what no longer serves you!

🔗 **Getting your hands caught in the cookie jar (easy on the processed goodies!)**
Okay, no judgement here; we all have our moments! But consistently indulging in those highly processed foods can leave you feeling sluggish, heavy, and energetically depleted. They often lack the radiant energy that nourishes your system. Think of it as trying to run your amazing machine on low-grade fuel – it's just not going to hum at its best.

🔗 **Getting on the sauce (excessive alcohol consumption)**
Okay, my friend, a little celebratory tipple now and then? Maybe part of the fun! But relying on alcohol to numb, avoid, escape, or just as a social lubricant? That's like trying to tune a beautiful instrument with heavy metal playing in the background. It can cloud your energy, mess with your natural

rhythms and sleep (hello, grumpy vibes!), blur your intuition, and generally lower your overall sparkle. Everything in moderation, right? Let's keep that inner light clear, bright, and connected!

∞ Being around energy vampires (negative people and groups)

You know those folks who seem to suck the life out of a room? Yeah, those people are the energetic equivalent of a bad Wi-Fi signal. Surrounding yourself with people or groups who consistently project toxic energy, gossip, complain, or engage in harmful behaviours is like trying to maintain your high vibe in a room full of buzzing negativity. Their chaos can really drain your energy, and before you know it, your own frequency starts to dip to match theirs. Choose your tribe wisely, my friend; surround yourself with those who lift you higher!

∞ Holding grudges is holding you down, sister

Clinging to resentment? Oh, honey, that's like carrying a messy, stinky, poo – hoping to toss it at someone. It only affects you. It also builds a heavy, low vibration inside, making it tough to move forward with any lightness or peace. Acceptance fits in here. Forgiving yourself and your part in a situation that caused pain is where relief begins. Letting go of resentment is like dropping that heavy bag and suddenly feeling free and able to dance! It's for your own good, mate, to let go and let your energy flow freely. (I don't necessarily endorse forgiving others in trauma experiences in the traditional sense; I support acceptance.)

∞ Your Former Self is talking negatively about you

Ouch! The way you speak to yourself has a profoundly direct impact on your vibration. Harsh self-criticism, that constant inner "mean girl", self-doubt, and those yucky feelings of unworthiness? That creates low and stagnant energy. Seriously, my friend, is it worth it? And, frankly, you don't deserve it. Treat yourself with the soothing tenderness

> **"The universe doesn't give you what you ask for with your thoughts – it gives you what you demand with your vibrations."**
> – Abraham Hicks

where all parts of yourself are welcome and understood. Your inner dialogue sets the tone for your energetic symphony.

Ultimately, my friend, *you* are the conductor of your vibrational orchestra! The way you treat yourself. The loving-myself actions you deploy. The pure kindness. The generous nourishment for both your mind and body. This is all about how you actively tune your inner instrument to a higher, more harmoniously connected frequency. When you engage in self-criticism, neglect, or surround yourself with negativity, you create an inharmonious inner world, and your vibration will reflect that.

Becoming aware of your vibration and consciously choosing to hone in on the influences that uplift it is an act of know-how and self-empowerment, and a MAJOR step forward in becoming liberated. It's about taking the reins of your inner instrument and creating a life that works for you. Where you sing in the shower, and metaphorically skip throughout the day. One where you feel groovy. Top of the world. A dazzling example of a life that resonates with joy and peace as a vibrant, gloriously authentic woman.

> Let's say, we agree: You are the composer of your own energetic symphony, my friend, and you absolutely have the power to create beautiful tunes. So go ahead; how about you have a crack at conducting your own masterpiece?!

A Note

A side bar between us girls ...

My friend, this is your time to slow things down. To observe. You're starting to notice that when you're grounded, shifts occur, aren't you? This is when you apply the knowledge that your energetic vibration is also connected to your emotions. So, instead of brushing them aside, be curious again about the message. You see, now, in your new capacity for change, you're better at navigating life's stressors – something truly worth observing. Watch yourself. See how you deal with potential triggers. With new skills, perhaps you're not just pushing through them, but by listening to your limits and honouring your needs.

> Being raw, honest, and true.

6. Hypervigilant Energy

The Unseen Armour
Understanding Hypervigilant Energy

If you're reading this, chances are, you know deep in your bones what it feels like to be constantly on guard, even when there's no apparent danger. You might recognise that subtle hum of anxiety that never seems to fade, that inner, incredibly subtle radar constantly scanning for potential threats and always feeling jumpy, always alert, even kind of suspicious to a fault. This, my friend, is often the imprint of trauma, a state we call hypervigilance, or what I think of as "hyper-attuned energy". Let me break this down for you so you understand the concept correctly.

🔍 Trauma and Hypervigilance

Survival Response: When a child experiences trauma – whether it's not having their needs met, various forms of mental or physical abuse, neglect, or witnessing violence – their brain can adapt to perceive the world as dangerous and unpredictable. Hypervigilance, a state of heightened alertness and sensitivity to the environment, develops as a survival mechanism to detect potential threats.

Brain Development: Trauma during critical periods of brain development can impact the areas responsible for threat detection (amygdala), memory (hippocampus), and emotional regulation (prefrontal cortex). This can lead to a nervous system that's easily triggered into a state of high alert. (Remember what we talked about in Book Two: *A New Perspective*, about the consequences of Adverse Childhood Experiences and the impact on proper brain development? This is all part of that.)

Lasting Impact: This learned hypervigilance can become ingrained, persisting into adulthood even when the individual is no longer in a dangerous environment. The brain remains primed to scan for threats.

> So, before now, had you heard the word "hypervigilance"? If you hadn't, don't worry. I didn't fully grasp the depth of it until later in life. Nevertheless, I always knew there was something different about me in how I reacted to things compared to other people. So, when I finally learned about it, the definition resonated with deep familiarity.

Understanding this aspect of ourselves, this heightened awareness born from past hurts, can be a powerful key in unlocking why we react the way we do, why certain situations can feel so overwhelming, and even how it can steer us towards choices with food and drink that don't really nourish us.

So, turn the not-so-pretty topic into something positive – think of your hypervigilance as an invisible armour you've had to wear, forged in experiences where you weren't safe, where your needs weren't met, or where trust was shattered. You did this to survive, my friend. Like I did, and that's okay. Come now, let's gently explore how this might show up in different ways.

> **"Trauma creates changes you don't choose. Healing is about creating change that you do choose."**
> – Michelle Rosenthal

Example One: The Child Whose Needs Weren't Met (Neglect)

Imagine a little girl whose cries for comfort went unanswered, whose hunger pangs were ignored, whose emotional needs were consistently overlooked. Her young nervous system learned a difficult lesson: The world isn't always a reliable place. No one is always coming to help. To survive, she had to become hyper-attuned to the subtle shifts in her environment – the tone of a caregiver's voice, the hurried footsteps that might signal a fleeting moment of attention, the silence that meant she was indeed alone – because at any moment, she could feel vulnerable again.

As an adult, this woman might exhibit hypervigilance in ways that seem perplexing to others, and even to herself. She might:

Constantly Seek External Validation: Because her needs weren't consistently met, she might perpetually look for reassurance and approval, her inner sense of worth feeling fragile and dependent on others.

Struggle to Relax: That ingrained sense of unease, the feeling that something is always about to go wrong, can make authentic relaxation feel impossible. Her body might be tense, her mind racing, even in seemingly safe environments.

Misinterpret Neutral Cues as Negative: A simple delay in a response or a slightly raised eyebrow could be perceived as rejection or abandonment, triggering intense emotional reactions rooted in early neglect.

Have Difficulty Identifying Her Own Needs: Having learned that her needs didn't matter, she might struggle even to recognise what she truly wants or needs in the present, prioritising the perceived needs of others instead.

Example Two: The Woman Abused by Her Partner

Consider a woman who lived with the unpredictability of, and fear from, an abusive partner (the abuse is something she didn't admit to outwardly). Her days were a tightrope walk, constantly assessing his mood, anticipating his triggers, and trying to navigate his volatile emotions to protect herself. Her nervous system became acutely tuned to the slightest change in his demeanour – a clenched fist, a sharp tone, a particular silence. Survival depended on this heightened awareness.

Even after leaving the abusive situation, this hypervigilance can linger, casting a long shadow. She might:

Be Easily Startled: A sudden noise, a raised voice (even in a neutral context), can trigger a wave of fear and anxiety, mirroring the unpredictable outbursts she once endured.

Struggle with Intimacy and Trust: Having been betrayed and harmed by someone she should have been able to trust, forming new intimate relationships can feel incredibly risky. She might be constantly scanning for red flags, even when none exist.

Have Difficulty Asserting Boundaries: Her boundaries were likely violated repeatedly, leaving her feeling powerless to say "no" or to protect her own space and needs in future relationships.

Experience Flashbacks and Intrusive Thoughts: Her mind might replay past traumatic events, keeping her locked in a state of fear and alert, as if the danger is still present.

> Even if these examples don't resonate with you, I wonder if this sounds like anyone you know?

🔍 The Toll of Hypervigilant Energy

This constant state of alert, this unseen armour, takes an immense toll on your entire being. It can disrupt your very vibration, keeping your nervous system in a state of chronic high alert, leading to physiological overload. Your body is constantly pumping out stress hormones, impacting everything from your digestion to your immune system.

Grounding becomes a significant challenge. When your system is wired for threat, settling into the present moment feels inherently unsafe. Your mind races, your body feels restless, and finding that inner anchor seems impossible.

Emotionally, hypervigilance can lead to dysregulation and disconnection. You might find yourself overreacting to small things, experiencing intense and uncontrollable emotions, or conversely, feeling numb and disconnected from your own feelings to cope with the constant intensity.

It fundamentally impacts your relationships, as the ingrained mistrust and fear can sabotage intimacy and create cycles of conflict. It erodes your trust in yourself, as your perceptions become filtered through the lens of past trauma, making it difficult to discern genuine intuition from fear-based reactions. And the constant state of alert inevitably disrupts consistent sleep, leaving you exhausted and even more vulnerable.

> **"In the midst of movement and chaos, keep stillness inside of you."**
> — Deepak Chopra

Trauma, Hypervigilance, and Anxiety

Because I suffered chronic anxiety over the years, when I discovered I was also experiencing hypervigilance, I wanted to investigate if the two were linked. And in short, yes, they are. Studies, medical research, my own psychologist, and my general practitioner all confirmed this. (Later, I found this also came up in all my psychological studies.)

Yes, my friend, there is a strong connection between childhood trauma, chronic hypervigilance, and anxiety. So, let me share with you how this often unfolds:

The Link Between Chronic Hypervigilance and Anxiety

- **Constant State of Alert:** Being chronically hypervigilant means the body and mind are constantly "on guard", as we explored earlier. Therefore, this sustained state of arousal triggers the body's stress response system, leading to chronic anxiety.

- **Physical Symptoms:** This can manifest in various physical symptoms of anxiety, such as increased heart rate, muscle tension, difficulty sleeping, sweating, and a heightened startle response.

- **Psychological Symptoms:** Constant threat detection also fuels worry, fear, and a sense of being on edge. It can make it difficult to relax, concentrate, and feel safe, contributing to generalised anxiety, panic disorders, and social anxiety.

- **Misinterpreting Cues**: Hypervigilance can cause individuals to misinterpret neutral or safe situations as threatening, further increasing anxiety levels. Subtle cues like a change in someone's tone or a sudden noise can be perceived as danger, creating more anxiety.

In essence, the way anxiety and hypervigilance are linked keeps the nervous system in a persistent state of threat response, which is a core component of anxiety disorders.

Later, I am going to share with you what I did to "calm the farm" within me and soothe my hypervigilance, cracking the code in my own language, and for my own lasting change. I haven't had an anxiety attack for a very long time, and I'd like to keep it that way.

Home: Not Always a Sanctuary

The home, ideally a sanctuary and safe haven where we can completely unwind, can sometimes, unfortunately, feel like anything but. For those of us with a history of trauma, our own living spaces can unknowingly harbour elements that trigger or worsen that hypervigilant feeling. It's like walking into a minefield sometimes, isn't it? These triggers can show up in many ways.

- **Unpredictability and chaos (frequent loud arguments or yelling, etc.):** It can feel like you're constantly waiting for the next explosion.

- **Inconsistent routines and schedules:** It's so hard to relax when you never know what's coming next.

- **Sudden, unexpected changes in the environment (constantly moving your belongings or even furniture):** It's like the ground keeps shifting beneath your feet.

- **A general sense of instability or lack of order:** When your external world is chaotic, it mirrors the chaos inside.

- **Sensory overload (constant loud noises, e.g., TV always on, loud music):** This can feel like an assault on the senses.

- **Overly bright or harsh lighting:** Sometimes, I just need a softer glow to feel at peace.

- **Strong or unpredictable smells (cleaning products, cooking odours):** Certain smells can bring back unwanted memories in a flash.

- **Clutter and disorganisation (making it hard to feel a sense of calm):** When your space is cluttered, your mind feels the same.

- **Lack of safety and security (actual threats present, e.g., ongoing abuse or neglect):** This is the most serious and needs addressing with appropriate support.

- **Feeling unsafe due to inadequate security (broken locks, living in a high-crime area):** Your home should be your sanctuary (or fortress), not a place of fear.

- **Reminders of past trauma within the home (certain objects, rooms, or layouts):** It's like walking past a trigger every day.

- **Emotional neglect or volatility (a lack of emotional awareness or responsiveness from parents/caregivers/housemates):** Feeling invisible or unheard at home is incredibly painful.

- **Sudden shifts in mood or unpredictable emotional reactions from others in the home:** It can feel like you are always on guard, like you're always bracing for impact.

- **A feeling of having to "walk on eggshells":** This phrase says it all, doesn't it?

- **Intrusions and a lack of boundaries (a lack of personal space or privacy):** You need a place that's just yours.

- **Others entering your room without permission:** This can feel like a violation.

- **Difficulty establishing and maintaining boundaries:** Saying "no" can be so hard, but it's so important.

Creating a trauma-informed home environment isn't about perfection; it's about being mindful of these potential triggers and actively working to establish safety, predictability, and calm. This might involve decluttering (even just a little bit at a time), establishing easy routines, using soft lighting, minimising loud noises, ensuring physical security, and fostering respectful communication and boundaries. It's about creating a space where your nervous system can finally take a deep breath and believe, genuinely believe, that it's safe to relax.

🔍 Finding Your Way Back to Calm

Here's the truth. This hypervigilant state, while a powerful survival mechanism, doesn't have to be your permanent reality. As you begin to connect with your inner self, to gently ground yourself in the safety of the present moment, to learn the art of setting boundaries that protect your energy, and to actively calm the chaos that might still echo from the past, you can begin to lower and soothe that hypervigilance.

It's a delicate process, a process of sending new messages of safety to your nervous system and brain. Each conscious breath, each boundary you assert, each moment you allow yourself to simply rest, is a step towards rewiring those ingrained threat responses.

> **"When parts of you are triggered, more rational and grounded parts may be overwhelmed and unable to make effective decisions."**
> – Suzette Boon

This journey isn't about erasing the past; it's about creating a present and a future where you are no longer held captive by the echoes of the past. It's about recognising that you are safe now, that you are strong, and that you have the power within you to shed that heavy armour, piece by delicate piece, and step into a life where your energy is no longer consumed by constant alert but flows freely towards joy, peace, and genuine connection.

You are worthy of this calm, and together, we will find the path.

7.
My Trauma Experience

Healing My Hypervigilance
Never Easy, But All Worth It to Change My Life

Right, first up, I need to tell you that I was incredibly hypervigilant but completely unaware of it. I had no idea that was the reason for my behaviour or what was happening to me. To be fair, despite the abuse I endured growing up from people and in places I should have been able to trust, as an adult, my life was also threatened several times by an unhinged family member.

After an argument on the phone about family money, he was very controlling, talking down to me and over me, telling me, "How it is." When I tried to set a boundary – being new to boundaries at the time – he would freak out, throwing abuse at me, putting me down, and calling me a "fuck-up." When I told him I wouldn't talk to him anymore if he kept treating me that way, he responded with a creepy Joker-like laugh and said, "Oh, you think you are so clever, don't you?" I repeated myself, and he lost it, his tone turning fierce, almost demonic. He then said he wanted to kill me. "I'm going to kill you, you little bitch!" I was stunned, completely frozen – just for a moment. He repeated it, "I'm going to fucking kill you. As soon as I get my hands on you, I'm gonna kill you." I hung up, feeling grateful I didn't live nearby, thinking that distance was my safety.

I spiralled after that. I attempted to seek support from other family members, and I was turned away. They didn't want to know about it. One even said he couldn't speak to me about it because it would trigger his own trauma, so I was on my own. A parent said, "Don't worry about it. You'll be fine." More gaslighting, more denial, and more making me out to be a drama queen. Indeed, there was no sign of an empathetic witness in sight.

The night after my father passed away, there was another fraught clash (I alluded to this in my last story). This time, I stood up for myself – but foolishly, this time I fought back on his level. I was forty-three then. When he started telling me "How it was" and belittling me, I expressed my feelings about him. Well, my rage took over. I called him the C word. I swore at him, returned the abusive name-calling, and told him to F off, too. I thought I was fighting back, defending myself, but unfortunately, it ended in disaster.

This act of defence led to me being pushed onto the corner of a cement step. When it happened, I couldn't feel my left leg. The man who did this to me ran away – fled, like a coward. The other family member told me to stop being such a drama queen. My Mother arrived and demanded I get into her car. Begging to be taken to the hospital, my injuries were dismissed. I was told I was fine, and certainly didn't need a medical treatment. There's no way my mother would let that happen; it would be far too embarrassing for the family.

> When I finally got X-rays taken, I discovered I had fractured my femur, hip, and sacrum. I developed necrosis of the femoral head (basically, it died due to lack of blood supply) and would require a hip replacement. My orthopaedic surgeon described my injuries as being equivalent to being pushed out of a ten-storey building; they were that serious. He couldn't believe this was caused by a man who, after all, was part of my family. This all became a three-year ordeal of chronic pain for me. I'll tell this story in more detail another time.

I was forced into my mother's car and taken back to the family farm, twenty minutes out of town. When I tried to leave in my hire car, another fight blew up. Trying to take my car keys, he became very forceful. I got bashed in the face, breaking my glasses in the process. I was stuck. No key, no mobile – he buried my phones (personal and work) in the garden. His wife had wrenched my handbag from my shoulder and thrown the contents of my bag, and all my makeup, over the garden. Somehow, in all the chaos, I called the police from the home phone, begging for help.

When I hung up, I was shamed and accused of causing this drama, so don't expect any sympathy. This man was relentless in his attacks on me. The abuse was being hurled again, while other family members just stood by and watched – t was me and three others in the room, all complicit in this abuse. I was the godmother of his children, and in the chaos of trying to get away from his grasp, I avoided another swing, and his rage escalated once more. He declared, in that same terrible, spine-chilling tone, "I'm going to kill you!" As he chased me around the sofa, trying to grab me, I was panic-stricken, constantly dodging him. Thank goodness for my quick legs, I can say. "Come here, bitch!" Another missed swipe. I broke free from his reach, and the home phone rang, halting the chaotic chase – it was the police at the front gate. He stopped and stared at me across the room. Enraged. I felt as if I were on the other side of a caged wild animal. He said, "You're done. You're fucking done, bitch. If you ever contact my kids again, I'm going to hunt you down and cut you into little pieces." I believed every word of it. When the police arrived, I felt like I could breathe, but the horror wasn't over.

> **"A person's a person, no matter how small."**
> – Dr. Seuss

I haven't spoken to him since, nor his beautiful children, who I loved and adored like they were my own. This whole encounter was unfathomably scary, all incredibly surreal, and yet, all very real. He was a man with deep anger and rage issues, having suffered complex trauma and abuse as a child himself. He was clinically diagnosed with several psychological disorders, and when off his medication, he was highly volatile. He had been arrested for bashing up a stranger and was regularly in fights. He would even kick his family dog in the stomach if in a rage, in front of his own children. So, there was no way of thinking these were empty threats. He, with all his past trauma driving his behaviour, meant what he was saying at the time.

> Just so you know, beyond my complicated and highly traumatic upbringing in childhood and my teenage years, I continued to encounter a series of abusive experiences in my adult life that kept me constantly on edge. This was one of the more extreme events that happened.

My hypervigilance was always a step ahead of me. My friends would tell me I was "super sensitive," and my family often dismissed me as a "drama queen," which was very triggering, mind you. I would jump at any sudden noise. I was always "on," and I found it very hard to sit down and relax. I constantly felt the need to be doing something. I was always hyper-aware of what was happening around me – who was there, what they were doing, and how close they were getting to me. I was far too alert. I suspected everyone, and I believe I studied people's body language as a way to protect myself. I lived with knives hidden in various spots around the house, just in case there was an unwelcome intruder or one of my family members came looking for me. It's sad to admit this, but I moved into a new house in 2024, and the protection kits went back into their hiding spots, once more.

I constantly suffered from tense muscles in my back – my massage therapist would say, "Geez, love, you could smash bricks against your back." I had trouble falling asleep and staying asleep, and I would wake up at any sound, familiar or not, throughout the night. I suffered from terrible anxiety, and if triggered, my face would turn bright red, my heart rate would skyrocket, and I would be a complete wreck. This was no way to live, and I knew I had to find a way to address the triggers that were fuelling my hypervigilant responses.

Moving Forward in Life

To cut a long story short, my initial strategy was to address two key issues affecting my life – proximity to chaos and environment/geography. I had to completely remove myself from the chaos and distance myself from the people who caused it. I also had to be honest and real about how the environmental factor also triggered my hypervigilance. Once I did those two things, I began to understand how they impacted my energy. It wasn't until I took these measures that I could start a holistic healing process. As you will recall, I talked about this in Book Two: *A New Perspective* – you can't begin to heal unless you feel safe. With these two significant steps taken, I embarked on a full-on mind, body, and environmental cleansing. Removing myself from the chaos created a space for me to explore my own energy. I didn't realise it at the time, but it was such a vital step in soothing my energy and opening the door to healing my hypersensitivity and hypervigilance.

Next, I went through a process of fundamentally examining my life and how I showed up in each situation. This was a confronting yet profoundly important exercise of taking responsibility for my role and actions in all the chaotic situations I had been in. I looked at the scenarios I was drawn to, the people who fed off my energy, and my role in each trigger. I set boundaries with my energy vampires, and, like clockwork, they started to disappear. (They really didn't like it when I wasn't available to "people-please" anymore.)

> **"You cannot find peace by avoiding life. You can find peace by confronting life within you."**
> – Dr. Wayne Dyer

You see, what I discovered was that I had created, connected with, and attracted a lot of energy vampires (people who can drain your energy). My role was often that of a people-pleaser, the counsellor, the therapist – listening to and supporting their chaotic life issues and relationships, often placating them to gain their love and acceptance. I was generous to a fault with my time, money, and food, giving all I had, all my precious energy, to take care of their needs and wants while neglecting my own. I carried a deep, murky well of resentment.

Being a people-pleaser is incredibly lonely. No one ever helped me or offered me support. No one ever cooked for me or bought me dinner as a thank you, as a way to reciprocate what I provided. They would often arrive at my house empty-handed and leave full, and usually drunk. I would wake up the next day not only hungover but also with a massive energy hangover. I had been trauma-dumped on, energy-dumped on, and had absorbed their often negative, messy, chaotic energy, which stuck to me like glue. (I didn't realise it was an energy hangover at the time; I learned that later.) But I kept showing up in these constant, chaotic scenarios that hurt my balance and activated my hypervigilance. I did that. I was actively and willingly getting involved in all these energy-draining situations.

The consequence was that the resentment I carried would turn into anger, which would then lead to more unwanted and destructive behaviours. I used these behaviours to deny the pain or to avoid taking responsibility for what I was doing – more drinking, more binge eating, more negative self-talk – because it was always about them, never about me. I came to realise that all that resentment was like carrying around a sloppy, stinky, poopy mess, hoping to throw it at someone else. It would never work; instead, it would drip all over me, leaving me smelling and feeling terrible, like the toilet-bowl mess I was carrying. It was time for me to take responsibility and own my actions. (Sorry for the unpleasant imagery there, but I needed to make a point!)

I will be honest, letting those people go was hard. It created a different kind of loneliness, one laced with fear. The old narrative, of taking ownership of a bad situation when it wasn't mine to take, crept in. The story I would tell myself is, "It must be something I've done." That old chestnut. But I kept reminding myself that my top three values were to be honest, to challenge myself, and to accept my current circumstances. With that, I rebuilt my life. And, as I say, it opened up some really wonderful doors to new connections I would never have found, had I not taken those necessary steps to walk towards my Future Self.

Then, I had to look at my living environment. I lived in an apartment block with loud neighbours who would party and have random guests through the night, often waking me in fear and startling me regularly. Drug deals often happened outside the garage door of the building or in the stairwell. The area was "funky" and "cool", but it didn't feel safe, with many homeless people seeking shelter in nearby streets. My kitchen was practically non-existent, with just a small benchtop and a tiny gas cooktop. It wasn't easy or fun to create meals.

My friends nearby were all heavy drinkers and were still using drugs on their nights out, which seemed to be more frequent than not. I didn't want to drink and certainly wasn't interested in drugs, so hanging out with them felt empty. I had to face the facts; we didn't want to do the same things anymore. It felt claustrophobic because we had been friends for years and lived close by, but I didn't relate to them anymore. Stepping outside that social norm was really tough. It was lonely and isolating, even living in such close proximity to my friends. There was also the hope that if I moved away, I would be further away from family members and could live anonymously, reducing the fear of more confronting (and life-threatening) events happening again.

This all happened in 2021, around the time COVID-19 lockdowns were still in place in Australia. It devastated many people, but it was good for me in many ways. It gave me the space to think about what I wanted from my life. I had to be honest with myself and ask, "Is this the lifestyle I want? Does my lifestyle align with my values?" The answer was a clear "No." The next question was, "Am I staying in this unhealthy lifestyle to keep up with the Joneses, to stay connected to people I once sought acceptance from?" The harsh truth was that there was no other reason to stay. It was obvious. If I wanted to become the woman I aspired to be and achieve the Future Self I had envisaged, significant change was necessary.

I made the brave decision to leave Melbourne and rent a small apartment on the Mornington Peninsula, just an hour's drive from the city, along the coast. By doing so, I successfully removed myself from the environmental triggers that heightened my hypersensitivity. I was just a five-minute walk to the peaceful waters of the sea, which I loved. Each morning, I'd walk along the beach to get a coffee, chat with locals, and exchange smiles instead of grunts from city dwellers. The community was friendly and welcoming.

I became anonymous for a while, not telling many people my address or exact location. I distanced myself from family members who were the root of my trauma. I also distanced myself from many who led chaotic lives or created chaos in mine. I removed myself from situations where I felt I had to play a role, which had caused

> **"What you deny or ignore, you delay. What you embrace and accept, you transform."**
> – Deepak Chopra

internal chaos. It wasn't easy to untangle those friendships. But I found that once I was honest with these people, stopped placating them, stopped telling them what they wanted to hear, and set clear boundaries about what I was willing and not willing to do, they all drifted away. This opened up space for new, genuine friendships. It was so wonderful to be truly seen – not judged, with no preconceived ideas about who I was or once was. Just being seen – appreciated for the woman I am today. Until I experienced this, I didn't realise how refreshing it was not to be constantly reminded of the past by people who needed me to stay anchored there because of their own stories.

I found peace when I did all that and set those boundaries. With less chaos and cluttered energy around me, I found a natural connection to my own energy and vibration, which made me curious to learn more. I felt this move was leading me to raise my energetic frequency. The hyperarousal and super-sensitivity began to dissipate, and the constant alert state practically disappeared. I began to meet and attract female energetic healers who taught me about the importance of energy, how to raise my vibration, and how to maintain my focus on my purpose.

This happened again after I fell down the stairs at work and badly damaged my back. I concluded that I was meant to fall, to meet these healers who guided and reminded me to tap into my inner voice to heal. I went from chaos to peace and experienced a different form of happiness. Not manufactured, no. A more pure, home-grown kind. The people I met were all different. Totally out of the norm, from where I had come from, and so refreshing. It was so liberating. It was such a different experience for me, and I loved it.

Don't get me wrong. I am still very aware of my surroundings, but the fear no longer controls me. I'm not constantly on guard. I'm no longer subconsciously waiting for someone to attack me.

The peace I've found, the beautiful energy I am consciously aware of every day, along with the beautiful hum of my vibration, has created a new harmony in my life. Harnessing and protecting my own lovely, soothing energy has been such a gift. Undoubtedly, removing the exhausting component of chaos was a game-changer. Sure, short-term pain, initially, but worth it all, for a lifetime of change.

If you're reading this and thinking, "Gosh, I feel like that," please know you're not alone. This is often a consequence of experiencing childhood trauma, abuse, or neglect – it's a part of the human condition. But you absolutely can switch from automatic back to manual, just like I did. Healing is realistically within your reach – I'm hoping you can see this now?

This is precisely why understanding and mastering your energy, finding your balance, and connecting to your source to fill your own cup is so incredibly vital.

> **"Be honest with who you are, why you want and how you want to be treated. Boundaries only scare off the people that were not meant to be in your life."**
> – Shannon L. Alder

> I wanted to share the truth about what I had to do in my life to heal myself. It may be very different for you – or you may find that the things I share really resonate.

8.
Yin and Yang

Healing and Liberation Hand in Hand
The Powerful Impact of both Feminine and Masculine Energy

Right, my friend, here is probably the best place to explain what I mean when I speak of Feminine and Masculine Energy. I will start by saying that this has absolutely nothing to do with your gender. Rather, we all have both energies within us, and they're like two complementary forces, working together. This, I hope you will come to appreciate, is part of everything falling into place.

Think of it like this: Your Feminine Energy – often called Yin – like I touched on in Chapter Four, is all about being receptive (or open to receive), intuitive (listening to the inner voice), and emotional (free to express, feel and sit with your emotions). It's your nurturing side, your creativity, and where you find your flow. It's about *being* – surrendering, feeling, healing, connecting, receiving, resting, and, would you believe, looking inwards. Your Masculine Energy, or Yang, is your active, logical, and (for the sake of explaining this to you) "structured" side. It's protective, direct, and focused, helping you with *doing*. Which means, taking action, setting boundaries, analysing things, being disciplined, assertive, leading, and ensuring safety. What is important here for you is finding that beautiful balance between the two that will help you understand yourself on a deeply connected scale. With your true, core, combined, deeply primal energy source. All part of your path to becoming more liberated.

For some of us, the mix of energies can be nicely balanced; for others, it's one-sided, or one side may appear to be more dominant. As you will learn and start to appreciate, for women like us who have experienced trauma, the Wounded (or Toxic) Masculine Energy can become the dominant. Acting as a shield and protector, often not even realising it.

🔍 The Wounded Survival Strategies

My friend, trauma – whether a single event or complex trauma from unmet childhood needs – often forces us to adopt wounded or "over-expressed" versions of our primal energies to survive. For a woman, this frequently shows up in two main ways.

Firstly, there's an over-reliance on using Wounded Masculine Energy, where you might feel you always have to be in control. Or you may have become subconsciously avoidant to survive, believing that feminine qualities like vulnerability and emotional openness are unsafe. Consciously or unconsciously, this will give you the appearance that you are independent. Addicted to work, or overachieving, lacking self-control and boundaries, which leads to experiencing burnout, or becoming unwell. Being obsessive with things or overly structured. Emotionally numb and disconnected. Excessively controlling, gracefully, or obviously. Finding it hard to unwind or fall asleep. The resistance to ask for – or accept – help is an undercurrent. Not able to take feedback or perceived criticism and becoming defensive, feeling like everything is an attack. The underlying survival mechanism is the notion: "If I stay busy and in control, I won't be vulnerable. I will create my own safety because I cannot rely on others."

> Could one, two or possibly all of these behaviours I talk about here be you?

Secondly, there's an over-reliance on Wounded Feminine Energy, which often means a deep disconnection from your personal power, leading to a state of passivity or co-dependency. This can manifest as a lack of boundaries, people-pleasing, an inability to say "no," emotional flooding, a victim mentality, self-sabotage, chronic comparison, and difficulty taking clear action. The survival mechanism in this case is: "If I am nurturing and passive enough, people will like me and not abandon or hurt me. I will sacrifice my needs to gain acceptance and love."

The Power of Healthy Energy

Healthy Feminine Energy is your creativity, emotional heart, empathetic, caring, loving, nurturing self. It's about trusting yourself, and this is where your Liberation Toolbox works its magic. It's about your self-expression, the loving-yourself-actions you pursue, grounded in your most authentic self. Your Healthy Feminine Energy also embodies what I call "Primal Wisdom" – essential for setting boundaries. This is the energy of genuine and justified anger – not the chaotic outburst of the Wounded Self, but the clear, firm "no" that safeguards your core. When your intuition detects a breach, this energy emerges as your Inner Warrior, giving you the clarity and emotional intensity needed to stand firm and defend your peace. Recognising this helps you see anger not as toxic, but as a signal that your boundaries are in place for protection. Healthy Masculine Energy, on the other hand, means holding emotional stability, presence, and the ability to listen and hold space. This is the side of your energy that offers clarity, decisiveness, problem-solving, and rational thought. It is your accountability and action centre. It means creating a safe space, standing in integrity, and setting and maintaining healthy boundaries.

With balanced and Healthy Masculine Energy, you can enjoy true independence. It's a safe space where you feel comfortable having autonomy, self-reliance, and standing firm in your truth. I also want to note that when you connect with healthy masculine energy, you are more likely to test your confidence. You will try, fail, fall over, get up again, and keep trying – always learning. It's your pragmatic side, focused on moving forward and working towards specific, clear, future-oriented goals. This is where discipline comes in, supporting you as you practise all these new skills I've shared across the three books in The Change Experience series.

Masculine Energy is also your protector, the one who shields your pain. But on the flip side, so is your Feminine Energy; it is your Warrior Princess, with strong intuition and a clear inner voice, protecting you from harm as well. There's a balance needed here.

Balancing Feminine and Masculine Energy (your Yin and Yang), my friend, is a powerful step in reclaiming your whole self after experiences that may have caused one or both energies to become wounded or over-relied upon for survival. For me, I was very one-sided for many years. My Masculine Energy was my dominant energy. Before starting my studies on Energy work in 2021 and getting up to speed with the correct energy lingo, I used to call it "Toxic Male Energy", unaware that it was related to my unresolved trauma.

The Root Cause of Wounded Masculine Energy

The Wounded Masculine is essentially a survival mechanism that develops in response to trauma, shame, or deep-seated fears – like the fear of abandonment, failure, rejection, not being worthy, or being seen as weak.

As a result of the trauma, the Masculine Energy creates an armour. It creates a false sense of safety and control by suppressing the vulnerable parts of yourself – often the Feminine, which seeks connection, love, and inner peace.

In this wounded state, there is a fear of feeling deep emotions, which are associated with the Feminine Energy, because feeling them is seen as a loss of control or a sign of weakness, which could be preyed upon. This is where the emotional disconnection comes in, from the Wounded Masculine core. As the Healthy Masculine Energy is about protection, logic, and structure the psyche often decides that the core Feminine Energy qualities of softness, vulnerability, and receptivity are dangerous. In this place, logic doesn't exist, only the narrative that has been created at the time of the event (your trauma experience). To survive, the mind unconsciously develops a Masculine Shield to suppress these Feminine Energy qualities. (This is the same theme as the "False Self" that I covered in the previous books.)

So, what does this look like for you, do you think? Don't worry, there is a set of thought-provoking questions at the end of the chapter for you to reflect on and answer that question for yourself.

🔎 The Wounded Feminine Energy

Here's a softer truth, my friend: I would like to help you see how the behaviours associated with this kind of energy are coming from a place of deep, suppressed trauma experience or unmet childhood needs. The isolating feeling of being hurt, unseen or unheard, or broken by someone else's actions. This is the Wounded Feminine Energy's desperate, almost primal attempt to be visible, finally, understood or tended to.

The body is used as a tool to create an external crisis that cannot be ignored. This shows up in repetitive illnesses. Falling sick, suffering a chronic condition that demands attention. It might manifest as addiction and/or impulse control issues that inevitably cause suffering. Those automatic coping mechanisms you have employed for so long. These behaviours – like using food, alcohol, substances, or risky actions – are attempts to numb feelings or seek validation that the Feminine Energy was denied in childhood.

It's also where body dysmorphia lives, where you see your physical form as something constantly needing modification, because the authentic you feels unacceptable or unsafe. It's painful, but please know, my friend, this was always your heart trying everything it knew to get the deep care it deserved. Your protective parts just used the only means they felt capable of creating a crisis you couldn't ignore.

There are trickier aspects of what Wounded Feminine Energy can look like, too. It can be hard to spot in ourselves or in people we love. It often comes down to two sides of the same coin.

Think about that person who is oh-so-nice, agreeable to a fault, always smiling, never says 'no' – but makes you feel a little uneasy because you know they're doing it to get something or to keep the peace. If you find yourself doing this, or know someone who does, you're seeing a strategy where the beautiful, innate feminine quality of flow and harmony gets twisted into manipulation. (I will explain this as though it is someone you know.) This is the Wounded Feminine Energy expressing a fear of rejection, and it's backed up by a repressed Healthy Masculine Energy – the ability to assert needs. This person has decided that their authentic self – their true needs and desires – isn't acceptable, so they put on a performance of "niceness" to subtly control outcomes and feel safe. They've essentially squashed their honest, assertive voice (their Healthy Masculine) and are using a fake, sweet version of the feminine to get what they want indirectly.

> I'm not pointing the finger, but I wonder if you've done this? I know I have done it in the past. I know a lot of people who have too, I might add. And they still do.

The Clincher: Authenticity Through Vulnerability

The real big-ticket item in healing the Wounded Feminine is the courage to embrace vulnerability, because you simply cannot have authenticity without it. Think of authenticity as showing up as your true, unfiltered self – and vulnerability as the *action* of allowing that true self to be seen. Crucially, vulnerability isn't about dumping your "deep dark secrets" on everyone; it's about sharing an honest part of your current experience. A feeling, a fear, or a joy, without the armour of performance or protection. It's the willingness to be seen imperfectly. When you share something genuine, you drop the emotional mask. This act signals to the other person, "I trust you with this part of me." And here is the magic of the Healthy Feminine Energy – your openness acts as an invitation.

When the other person truly receives this without judgement – without using that information against you – they often instinctively respond by sharing a piece of their own truth. This mutual exchange of humanity creates a powerful, new kind of bond. A genuine, heart-to-heart connection that validates both people. This capacity for deep, relational connection is why cultivating Healthy Feminine Energy is so vital for you.

It turns the journey of change into a rewarding path of self-discovery, allowing you to finally experience the rich, reciprocal intimacy you were always meant to have.

> Can you see how all this talk about living in an authentic state needs some work – the ability to feel safe in your vulnerability is huge part of this picture.

The Energetic Body
Used as a Weapon or Armour

The concept that you use your body as "weapon" or "armour" is another layer in how trauma impacts your adult life today. Another aspect to consider when you are working on transitioning into the Healthy Feminine-Masculine Energy state of being.

The body is the primary site where trauma is experienced, stored, and defended against. When a person is unable to fight or flee (common in childhood trauma or single-event trauma), the energy of that trauma gets trapped in the nervous system, leading to involuntary physical and psychological defences. You may already know this, so nod if you do.

🔍 The Body as Armour (Inner Child Protection)

What we're talking about here is your body literally building a fortress to survive. That Armour is a defensive mechanism designed to prevent any further pain, saying to the world, "Go away, don't hurt me, please don't come closer."

It's the very core of the Wounded Masculine Shield, where your protective side prioritises rigid control over the soft, fluid connection your Feminine Energy heart truly craves. This is the Masculine Energy taking over, entirely convinced that structure and control are the only paths to safety.

For example, in relation to unmet needs, let's say you've experienced emotional neglect. The armour then becomes a refusal to receive. This is a denial of your Feminine Energy capacity to flow and accept help or love. You are not used to receiving love, support, or even simple kindness without a cost, so it becomes scary. That's why you might carry chronic tension in your jaw and shoulders, have a short temper with people, or hold a "stiff upper lip" posture that physically resists vulnerability and emotional flow.

If your trauma stemmed from a terrifying single event, or "perceived" life-threatening event (in your eyes), your Masculine Energy forces you into hypervigilance. This manifests as chronic tension in your diaphragm and shallow breathing, limiting your access to your emotions (the Feminine Energy realm). Why? Because your system is terrified of letting go of control. Being out of control means pain, suffering, and a "perceived" threat to your very life. Breathing deeply and relaxing the shoulders; it is not easy. Subconsciously, these feel like acts of surrender, which your inner protective armour cannot risk.

> "What you resist not only persists, but will grow in size."
> – Carl Jung

And, my friend, if you've experienced horrifying sexual trauma, the rejection of the sensual, receptive Feminine Energy form becomes a protective Masculine Energy disguise. I want to break this down more for you.

- **The Armour's Protective Ways:** When the body, which is naturally receptive – meaning it's built to feel, to receive touch, pleasure, and sensation (Feminine Energy), was the site of the violation, your armour concludes that receptivity is dangerous. Your internal protector (the Masculine Energy) then steps in to reject the physical shell.

    Think of it like this: If you touch a hot stove, your brain instantly creates a hard rule: *Touching the stove equals pain.* After trauma, your Inner Protector Armour (the Masculine Energy) creates

> "We all have an unsuspected reserve of strength inside that emerges when life puts us to the test."
> – Isabel Allende

Yin and Yang | 83

a similar, urgent rule: Being open, soft, or receptive to others equals vulnerability and danger.

- **The Result:** This often leads to disembodiment (you literally check out of your own body), or a fierce impulse to manipulate your shape to be less visible, less attractive – things like extreme haircuts, clothing, or weight gain or loss. Anything to create a shell that discourages the world from seeing or touching the true Feminine Energy within. The protective armour doesn't care that this rule stops joy; it only cares that it stops pain. Therefore, it locks down your capacity to receive, creating the armour to keep you safe from the terrifying possibility of being open again. My friend, your body becomes a structure for defence rather than a vessel for pleasure and joy.

> Can you see how this armour (Masculine Energy), though born from a desire to save you, is rooted in pain and suffering from your internal trauma narratives, ultimately locking the essential, soft Feminine Energy inside?

The Body as a Weapon for Punishing Yourself

Then there's the truly heartbreaking defence, my friend, where your body becomes a weapon used to punish the shame that resides deep within yourself. This is the crucial link between internalised trauma, shame, and external self-punishment.

This occurs when we turn that Trauma Energy inward, typically through self-sabotage, cruel self-talk, or destructive behaviours. It's utterly driven by shame and the core belief that "I am bad" or "I deserve this pain." This whole destructive loop is the Wounded Feminine Energy expressing her profound pain through the strict, critical actions of the Wounded Masculine Energy.

🔍 Manifestations of Internalised Shame

If you struggle with internalised shame, the Weapon is wielded through constant negative self-talk and judgement. These horrible, mean, and cruel criticisms create a daily psychological barrage. If you struggle with this, the mirror can become a genuinely dangerous place, reflecting not reality, but the severe inner critic.

This tragic expression of Wounded Masculine Energy can manifest physically as chronic illness flare ups – kicked off by any number of your personal triggers from the past, or simply even stress. This is often referred to as a "Body of Evidence Energy" – a subconscious, desperate expression that says to the world, "Look, see, I am a victim," or "I am sick, and I need attention." The body is used to articulate an invisible suffering.

Extreme behaviours like relentless exercising, denying yourself food, binge eating and purging, or rigorous dieting are also manifestations of this inner war. None of these actions are truly healthy for your body, yet you persist in pushing your physical form far past its limit as a distorted form of control.

> How is your health? Have you ever experienced a decline in your health when are feeling wounded?

 ## Balance and Integration: Your Internal Safety

Why do you need to understand and harness your Feminine and Masculine Energy, and how they work together?

The most quintessential reason why you, as a woman who has come this far, done all of these exercises, and invested all this time into healing your past, is because now you are ready to look at the next layer of evolution – the next step towards your *Liberated Connection*.

Understanding and harnessing the dynamic between your Feminine and Masculine Energy is where the integration of your core self – your authentic self – can finally be complete, within the safe space you have created. This space, my friend, is built through the work you've already done healing your Inner Child, reprogramming your neural pathways, and creating new narratives that are factual, align with your values, and look towards your Future Self.

> **"The integrated life is the real hallmark of an authentic adult. You are what you do, not what you say you believe."**
> — Richard Rohr

All of these exercises, reflections, and strategies for your healing and transformation are processes that demand vulnerability and deep emotional truth (this is your Feminine Energy). But for you, I want to acknowledge, a woman resolving unhealed past wounds, vulnerability feels like the greatest threat. So, give yourself permission to take your time with this.

So, the quintessential reason you need to understand both energies is to consciously rebuild an internal structure: your new narratives, core values, and clear vision of who you want to be and the life you want to explore. This is the Healthy Masculine, strong enough to safely hold the vulnerable, intuitive process (the Healthy Feminine) that leads to the authentic adult life you desire.

Here is the breakdown of why this integrated balance is non-negotiable for true healing and your Liberated Connection:

See the Masculine Energy as the Protector, not the Prison

As we discussed, trauma forces a woman to adopt the Wounded Masculine as a rigid armour. This armour's function is to create a false sense of control and safety. All the consequential behaviours that I have outlined previously are not coming from your core authentic self – meaning you are not being true to yourself either.

- **The Problem:** The shield keeps the world out, but it also keeps your authentic self – your Healthy Feminine Energy – locked in. It prevents you from accessing your true intuition, your capacity for flow, and your ability to receive love and support.

- **The Transformation:** By understanding the Healthy Masculine, you can dismantle the Wounded Masculine shield and replace it with a conscious space you hold inside. This space is characterised by firm boundaries, healthy discipline (e.g., ensuring you take time out and practise your new skills), and decisive action taken on behalf of your needs for a place of peace. This healthy, protective structure says: "I create the safety here, so you (my vulnerability) can finally be safe."

Your Feminine Energy (emotions, intuition, flow) is the primary source of where you will connect to your internal power. It's where you experience your inner voice, healing wisdom, and the blueprint for your liberated adult self.

- **Your Role:** To heal the past, you must allow yourself to feel the stored pain, trust your intuition over old programming (your new narratives), and receive the love you deserve. These are all pure acts of Feminine Energy at play.

- **Your Evolution:** Your healing truly begins when your Healthy Masculine steps up to hold the space for this process. Allowing your Masculine Energy to provide the structure and routine (the *doing*) so your Feminine Energy can dive into the emotional work (the *being*). Another example to bring this home:
    - **Feminine Insight:** "I need to heal my Inner Child."
    - **Masculine Response:** "I will block off Saturday morning, turn off my phone, and create a safe, uninterrupted space for this meditation."

> This may seem like I am repeating myself, but I want to emphasise this point so you truly understand the integration aspect. The main message I want you to take from this is that the Feminine Energy holds the key to your liberation.

In essence, the quintessential reason is that the unhealed woman uses the Wounded Masculine to *survive*, but the new you, a woman who accepts herself and all her colours and past experiences, uses the Healthy Masculine to create the safety required for your Feminine self to *thrive* and fully express who you are meant to be. Without this integration, you can remain powerful but perpetually armoured, protected but disconnected from the joy, connection, and authenticity you seek.

> Can we see how all these layers are now fitting together? And can you see how there is a need for three books to break all this down, piece by piece, so you can arrive at this place?

Balance Your Feminine and Masculine Energy
Breaking It Down for You to Try

Right, my friend, the key to finding balance after trauma is to heal those wounded parts of yourself and truly integrate the healthy, primal forms of both your Feminine Energy and Masculine Energy. Ultimately, it's about creating safety within your body so you can finally feel and receive.

First – Harnessing Your Healthy Feminine

To allow your Healthy Feminine Energy to emerge, focus on prioritising being over doing. For instance, set aside time without any agenda, simply to sit or do something uncomplicated. You might sit and gaze out the window at the world passing by, observe people – or watch the world from a café, or just sit in your garden listening to the birds and appreciating the beauty.

The Feminine Energy is fundamentally about learning to receive and trusting that it is safe to do so. For example, accepting a simple compliment like, "you look nice, " or "you did a great job." If you don't immediately find the words to respond, try to smile in acknowledgement. How about taking the first serve at dinner, or the last one if you're hungry? Feeling comfortable allowing someone to hold the door open for you to walk through first – how many times have you stood back and insisted that someone walk ahead of you? All that stuff you haven't allowed yourself when you've felt small. Why? Because this is the reprogramming, the retraining of your brain to understand that receiving is safe and nourishing.

You can also connect with your Healthy Feminine Energy through creative outlets. Grab a paintbrush and an inexpensive canvas, and paint something that makes you happy. Draw whatever you see – who cares how good or bad it looks? Or, with all this journaling you're doing, let your writing flow freely. Bake a four-layer cake with fun decorations and share it with friends. Or try cooking something new and different from a recipe book or an Instagram post. My favourite activity, which I do all the time, is dancing – shaking my tail feather every time I'm in the kitchen or garden. I love it; it feels so good! Truly, any gentle, non-punishing movement works. The wonderful gift of walking and spending time in nature helps you listen to that inner voice – your Primal Feminine Energy guidance. I'll teach you some practical techniques later in the book, so stay tuned.

> "You are imperfect, permanently and inevitably flawed. And you are beautiful."
> – Amy Bloom

SO, THE MESSAGE HERE IS THIS: These things – whatever they are for you – you need to do once, and then do it again. And again. Then some more. Repeat over and over until the shift comes. You will feel it inside, I promise you that.

Next – Activating Your Healthy Masculine

For your Healthy Masculine Energy – for those times when your boundaries have been violated or life has felt chaotic – this energy steps in as a loving protector.

It's about establishing and enforcing boundaries, my friend, truly deciding what's acceptable and acting to uphold it – even if it's just practising saying "no" without guilt. In the following few chapters, I will provide more detail about boundary work and teach you how to set and maintain them.

Yin and Yang | 89

You can also use this energy to create a gentle, predictable routine, like a regular bedtime or dedicated loving-yourself-action time, to bring structure to your world. This is all to reprogram the brain and change those old narratives that are on repeat.

And finally, it's about mindful action and assertiveness: learning to speak your truth clearly and kindly, using facts and logic not for control, but to make choices that ensure you are living by your values and taking care of your needs.

> **"The greatest thing in the world is to know how to belong to oneself."**
> – Michel de Montaigne

Finally – The Conscious Balance and Flow

Remember, balance doesn't have to mean a clean 50/50 split, not in this case anyway. One day it may be a 70/30, Masculine Energy to Feminine Energy, then the other way around. It all depends on what you are dealing with and what you need to ensure you are safe – consciously taking care of yourself – and that the path to peace and joy isn't overtaken by chaos. It's that conscious flow between the two, activating whichever energy you need in the moment.

I will say it again: by allowing your Primal Masculine Energy to create a safe, clear space (structure, boundaries, self-protection), your Primal Feminine Energy can finally feel safe enough to flow (be intuitive, vulnerable, and creative). And, you guessed it, allow your inner voice to be heard.

Three key elements to make sure this flows smoothly for you are:

1. **Self-Awareness:** Regularly check in with your emotional and energetic state: "Am I rushing to do it because I'm avoiding a feeling (Wounded Masculine Energy)? Or am I collapsing in inaction because I'm afraid to take a clear step (Wounded Feminine Energy)?"

2. **Non-Judgemental Observation:** Acknowledge your default patterns without shame. Simply recognise, "Ah, I'm trying to

control the outcome again. My inner Masculine Energy is trying to protect me." Thank that protective part, then gently choose a new response. The "Name and Tame Technique" works here beautifully as well.

3. **Letting the Energies Speak to Each Other:**
   - **The Feminine Energy** receives an intuitive insight ("I need more me time").
   - **The Masculine Energy** sets the structure and takes action to honour that need ("I will block my diary as unavailable next weekend").

My friend, reading and letting all this information sink in is another brave step forward. What we are doing here is giving light to your Healthy Masculine Energy, uncovering the protective shadows your mind created. But the next step – the one that requires the soft courage of your Feminine Energy heart – is to see these patterns within yourself.

I won't lie, this can feel a little hard at first. Then, as you really start to feel your healthy Feminine energy flow, ego subsides and makes this a whole lot easier. It's an act of honesty. A form of love language to yourself, and a way to look at the armour and weapon you built within, and realise it's a heavy load, and you no longer need it to survive.

> **"If you do not express your own original ideas, if you do not listen to your own being, you will have betrayed yourself."**
> – Rollo May

After the questions, I want to show you exactly how these energies played out in my own life – how I mistook my toxic control for strength, and how I finally found the grace to lay down my armour and weapon and soften back into my truest, authentic, and vulnerable self.

What do you say, are you ready to acknowledge your own armour and weapon, do the work and feel what it's like to let it go?

❓ Questions to Ask Yourself
An Honest Look Within

Alright, first, let's take a deep breath in and out together. Push your feet into the floor, sit up straight, and take another deep breath in and out. And again. Get yourself ready to read these questions so you feel grounded and prepared.

This next part requires you to feel grounded so you can truly absorb it and discover your truth. It's your time for honest, unfiltered self-exploration, in your safe space. No one else is here but you, these pages, and me – your steadfast cheerleader and guide.

You've done the vital work of learning about wounded and healthy energies. Now, to allow the wisdom to truly sink in, we need to bridge the gap between knowing and doing. This involves gently examining how these energies are currently manifesting in your life.

I'm going to ask you a series of questions. Don't rush. Take your sweet time. Let the feelings come. The goal is to evoke your own deep, compelling reasons for change.

> Slowly working through these is total okay.
> Read the questions aloud, then listen for
> the voice within to speak to you. It will
> come. Be patient, my friend. It will come.

Let's Begin

Part One: The Cost of Holding Wounded Energy

I want you to examine the impacts of your current behaviour here. These questions are designed to help you identify and visualise the gap between what you are doing now – your current state – and what aligns with your new values.

Connecting the Energy to Your Everyday Life

1. When you think about the Wounded Masculine Energy – that urge to push, control, or detach – what does that actually look like when you show up for your day? Picture it: Are you sitting silently but seething in a work meeting, or with family or friends? Are you just too busy to ever sit down?

2. And when you notice your Wounded Feminine Energy awakening – the urge to merge, manipulate, or play small – how does that show up? Describe the feeling: Is it a persistent, low-level anxiety about being liked? Is it a fear of speaking up that causes you to silently resent others?

3. On a scale from 1 to 10, with 10 being extremely exhausted, how tired are you from maintaining the role of being wounded – such as frequently getting sick, being hyper-independent, trying to please others, being super-nice, or always 'on'? If you rated yourself highly, what would a "5" on that scale feel like instead?

Exploring the Price You're Paying

1. Reflect on how you've used control (Wounded Masculine) or niceness/people-pleasing (Wounded Feminine) to feel safe. What is the true, hidden cost of that behaviour (your survival tactic)? What valuable parts of your life might it be taking away? For example, is it costing you a deeper connection with your

partner or friends? Is it costing you your peace of mind? Is it costing you your truth?

2. That persistent insistence on always being busy, always needing to do something – what are you skilfully avoiding when you refuse to slow down and simply be? What is the quiet truth you don't want to face?

3. How has your ability to resist your emotions – to be detached or unavailable – affected the people you love most? If they could write one honest sentence to you about it, and do so anonymously, what would it be?

4. In what ways has normalising chaos and drama become a comfort zone for you? What might you risk losing if you decided to embrace peace and stability instead?

5. What is the cost to your future self? If nothing changes in the next five years, what is the biggest disappointment or regret you can already see because of these wounded behaviours?

Part Two: Turning Towards Change

Now, I want you to shift your focus from the problem to the solution, creating a new kind of self-efficacy – a place where you trust and believe in your ability to change. Here are some steps for you to explore.

Imagining Your Healthy Self

1. When you stand powerfully in your Healthy Masculine Energy (the energy of direction, protection, and discernment), how do you want to show up in your daily life? What's the smallest behavioural change you'd notice first?

2. Reflect on a time when you feel passively or directly aggressive. What would a healthy, honest boundary look like instead? What is the one sentence you would say?

3. When you fully take time out, rest, and trust in your Healthy Feminine Energy (the energy of receiving, intuition, and flow), what does an evening at home look like? How do you feel in your body?

Your Commitment

1. You've just read about the powerful benefits of living in your Healthy Energies. On a scale of 1 to 10, how important is it for you right now to start shifting these behaviours? If your answer is less than a 10: What needs to happen for it to go from, say, a 6 to an 8?

2. What is the smallest, most manageable shift you could commit to this week that would signal to your soul, "I am choosing my Healthy Energy"? (e.g., a fifteen-minute me-time, slow-down, or asking for help on one small task.)

3. Imagine you succeed in making this small shift. What valuable thing does that one action enable you to gain or feel?

This is the power of turning inward, my friend. Your Wounded Energy is simply a loud protection mechanism, and it's kept you stuck. But you have the inner resources to choose a different way.

> So, I am curious. What do you choose now?

...

After the Questions

That was deep, powerful work you just finished. Please, take a deep breath. It's completely normal to feel a lot stirring — a mix of clarity, discomfort, and perhaps a little exhaustion from seeing your own behaviour and the price you're paying so clearly.

"A new consciousness is developing which sees the unity between opposites."
– Carl Jung

I want you to know that you don't need to analyse or solve anything else right now; the most important work is done. The simple act of creating that picture of the gap, of imagining what peace would feel like, has already sparked a shift within you.

So, take a well-deserved, proper break. Make a cuppa, something warm and soothing, rest your feet, and let all that quiet truth you uncovered gently settle.

> In your own way, allow it all to
> wash over you for a while.

🔍 Your Bonus Reflection:
The Change Experience Energy Balance
The Balance of Action (Masculine) and Being (Feminine)

If you took that break I suggested, well done you, and welcome back. This next part might be really eye opening. But first, let's pause for a moment and honestly acknowledge how far you've travelled! The heart of every exercise, emotional release, and vital insight you've gained from The Change Experience series stems from the dynamic interaction between your Masculine (action) and Feminine (being) Energies.

I wanted to take this a step further: to clearly show how all the beautiful work you've been doing connects to each of these energies. I've carefully assigned every action, activity, process, and commitment you're making to either the Feminine or the Masculine, ensuring clarity. As you read this section, see if your new understanding matches what you find.

> **"If any human being is to reach full maturity, both the masculine and the feminine sides of the personality must be brought up into consciousness."**
>
> – Mary Esther Harding
> (Carl Jung Student)

This is also a powerful reminder of the huge amount of work you've accomplished – and that's certainly not to be overlooked.

Yin and Yang | 97

Let's Begin

Here are the elements you've learned, and the core energy that drives them. The items assigned to Masculine Energy give you the clarity, structure, and protective action you need. The items assigned to Feminine Energy give you the intuitive wisdom, emotional truth, and inner connection required for liberation.

Element: The Action You Will Take	Core Energy
Acknowledge and accept your current use of automatic coping mechanisms	Feminine Energy
Educate yourself on trauma and its impact on your nervous system	Masculine Energy
Commit and do the work necessary to heal and process your past	Masculine Energy
Define and visualise your desired Future Self and destination (the life you truly desire)	Masculine Energy
Set daily intentions to consciously call in what you desire from the universe and set a positive tone for your day	Feminine Energy
Unpack your past family-of-origin influences on current life choices	Masculine Energy
Re-establish your current, authentic core values	Masculine Energy
Track and observe your patterns using a food diary	Masculine Energy
Implement a plan to improve your sleep hygiene	Masculine Energy
Reflect and be honest about using food or alcohol (or drugs) to numb pain or stress	Feminine Energy
Listen to your body and give it the specific nourishment and rest it is asking for	Feminine Energy
Take care and protect the routine that ensures 8 hours of sleep	Masculine Energy

Element: The Action You Will Take	Core Energy
Use the Strategies and take decisive action to reduce stressful situations	Masculine Energy
Journal to reflect on your current energetic presence and how you're showing up	Feminine Energy
Journal to process and articulate responses to reflection questions	Feminine Energy
Define your personal meaning of emotional resilience	Masculine Energy
Process and connect to the feelings related to unmet childhood needs	Feminine Energy
Be radically honest about your unmet childhood needs, or your Adverse Childhood Experiences (ACEs) and their current impact	Feminine Energy
Identify and journal the moments you lacked an empathetic witness	Feminine Energy
Practise the meditation to become your own empathetic witness and heal your Inner Child	Feminine Energy
Define and articulate your personal expression of anger today	Masculine Energy
Experience anger in its purest form, and recognise the place of its origin is a place to heal	Feminine Energy
Recognise that every emotion you experience holds an important message	Feminine Energy
Feel the sense of freedom that allows emotions to flow in and out without losing yourself	Feminine Energy
Practise and implement must-have life skills for emotional self-regulation	Masculine Energy
Implement grounding techniques (such as Name and Tame, Dropping Anchor, or 4-7-8 breathing) when life becomes overwhelming	Masculine Energy

Element: The Action You Will Take	Core Energy
Define and articulate your personal expression of anger today	Masculine Energy
Identify and list your quick-fix temporary high habits	Masculine Energy
Identify and map out your repetitive behavioural cycles	Masculine Energy
Understand and name your personal emotional triggers	Feminine Energy
Articulate and map out your trigger–behaviour–consequence loop	Masculine Energy
Complete and read aloud the reflection exercises to understand your emotions	Feminine Energy
Identify and name any individuals in your life who gaslight you	Masculine Energy
Use your knowledge of gaslighting phrases to protect yourself and assertively remove yourself from a triggering situation	Masculine Energy
Unmask and replace old narratives, rules, and judgements with new factual truths	Masculine Energy
Practise and integrate the Liberation Toolbox: self-trust, self-empathy, breathwork, and acceptance	Feminine Energy
Learn, practise, and implement clear, healthy boundaries	Masculine Energy
Identify and distance yourself from energy vampires in your life	Masculine Energy
Connect and appreciate the liberating power of your core energy source	Feminine Energy
Practise 'Forest Bathing' (walking in nature) to ground yourself and feel the earth's restorative energy	Feminine Energy

Element: The Action You Will Take	Core Energy
Proactively commit to practising skills and strategies to heal and keep moving forward. Knowing this is your life's work.	Masculine Energy
Explore the creative parts of yourself, and develop unrealised talents and interests	Feminine Energy
Appreciate the comfort and peace of living without constant inner chaos	Feminine Energy
Build new relationships with people who share and honour your core values	Masculine Energy
Allow yourself to feel safe when you choose to be vulnerable	Feminine Energy
Enjoy life by finding genuine happiness and contentment from within	Feminine Energy
Allow yourself to make mistakes and learn from them without self-judgement	Feminine Energy
Be proud of yourself, even when things are not perfectly executed or achieved	Feminine Energy
Catch yourself when you fall, and give yourself the validation you need to hear	Masculine Energy
Smile from the inside, knowing you are continually evolving as a woman	Feminine Energy
Find and appreciate the joy present in simple things and moments	Feminine Energy
Trust yourself and listen closely to your inner voice and intuition	Feminine Energy
Fall in love with the woman that you are today. A true love grounded in acceptance.	Feminine Energy

• • •

To Wrap This Up

This comprehensive list acts as your powerful visual blueprint of the energy dance for living a more liberated and connected life. See how you bring the Masculine Energy to enact change, balanced by the Feminine Energy vulnerability that allows your heart and body to genuinely heal. This harmony of the two is incredibly powerful, truly life-changing. When you fully embrace this understanding and its meaning with sincere appreciation, you'll find everything naturally falls into its beautiful, effortless rhythm.

> Now, take a deep breath, my friend,
> well done, you've truly done the work.
> You've just connected the dots!

9. My Wounded Energy Experience

My Fairly Unsexy Story
The Real Imbalance of Masculine vs Feminine Energy

I hope it's now clear that trauma often causes a woman to over-rely on Wounded Masculine Energy as a way to survive. Yes? Well, I was no different. I learned from my painful experiences that Feminine Energy qualities like vulnerability and emotional openness were a complete no-go zone.

For me I was highly independent, addicted to my work, and I based my life on a rigid, controlled structure, with little ability to accept anyone else's way. As you know from Book One: *Project Clarity*, I was extremely good at numbing my emotions, and it was impossible for me to ask for help. Perfectionism, always being "on," and a repetitive cycle of burnout were my norm. Exhausting, hey? All because my dear little Fleury inside wanted to avoid any more vulnerability and any more humans that would cause her pain.

For many years, I was incredibly one-sided in my energy. As I said before, my Masculine Energy was dominant. I used to call it "Toxic Male Energy", unaware that it was so deeply tied to my unresolved trauma.

The Reign of the Wounded Masculine

I was always so focused, goal-oriented, logical (in my mind), and incredibly pragmatic (in my perception of the world). At work, my style was warm and friendly, but very direct in my language. I wouldn't sugar-coat anything – "Tell them how it is" was my imprinted, family of origin, mantra. Delivering an honest, almost clinical truth that some people would love, but others, not so much. At times, female colleagues would tell me I could be rather harsh, looking for more softness from me – a side of myself I struggled to connect to. Equally, I could never apologise, or take responsibility for my role in anything, no way. Pure Wounded Masculine Energy right there.

On the flip side, I saw any kind of feedback as a massive blow – a sign of my unworthiness and being unlovable. I struggled to accept constructive criticism because it felt like a personal attack and a form of rejection. So, you know what I would do? I would reject them before they could reject me. And I would reward their helpful insight into my behaviour with a cold shoulder.

Close friends would plead with me to slow down – to take it easy – not to go so fast and hard at everything. "Stop and smell the roses," Ella, a gorgeous friend living with me in London, once said. "Whoa there, sister!" But you see, my friend, I couldn't. My body was in flight and fight mode. Being busy meant I didn't have to sit with myself in silence and feel what was happening underneath the surface. I didn't have to sit in emotional reality if I was always doing something.

I was addicted to the hustle at work, always taking on so much. A committed "good corporate citizen" in full flight, driven by a fear of not measuring up, hoping that these accomplishments would make me lovable. I worked ridiculous hours in overtime, long into the night on conference calls, often leading me to fall in a heap, sick, or completely numb from burnout. Horrible. As this was all in vain of gaining recognition from my core family or loved ones, which, sadly, never came.

I didn't trust myself. I didn't listen to my gut, ever. I certainly didn't take care of myself, treating my body like a machine that wouldn't break down. My attitude was that if I got sick, I'd take a pill and keep doing the same old stuff. And I got sick a lot, and I really suffered. Every time something was upsetting me, boom, I was in bed, unwell. I couldn't connect to my emotions, and I certainly couldn't speak about them. I had no idea what was truly making me so sick. Outwardly, I was very assertive and strong, but deeply closed off.

My control freak side, my unrelenting need to micromanage situations – that was incredibly powerful Wounded Masculine Energy. To have control meant I was safe; I knew what was happening next. My history was all about being hit out of the blue, loved one minute, hated the next – adored one day, abused the next. Inconsistency meant pain to me. Control meant strength. Protection. I fundamentally believed I couldn't rely on others, so my Masculine Energy took the reins.

Here's the thing, my friend: I used so many of those quick-fix, temporary highs I talked about in this book series to control and numb my emotions. I was then avoidant of people who tried to care about me and recoiled into isolation – all classic Wounded Masculine Energy traits.

I used to chase emotionally unavailable men, but the truth was, I was the one who was unavailable and energetically bankrupt. I had a deep fear of intimacy, avoiding commitment because then I'd need to rely on someone and be vulnerable with them. My Masculine Energy simply wouldn't allow me to be dependent on anyone.

What also helped me mask this deficiency was my "Miss Fix-It Syndrome." Always wanting to fix everyone else's problems, but never my own. It was my magnificent distancing effect. Showing up all loving and concerned, but never, ever, letting anyone in to see my mess bubbling away underneath. Again, Wounded Masculine Energy at its best.

My drinking would turn my suppressed emotions into a volcano, spewing out hot, dangerous flows of anger and rage, aimed at any male that had potentially done something wrong, or maybe got too close to me. Again, very Wounded Masculine. Then I'd shroud myself in shame, reminding myself that I was indeed a woman, and this kind of anger wasn't right, or so I believed.

I was chronically emotionally rigid. I had the most cruel and nasty inner critic who, no matter what I did, would find a fault or a flaw in how I looked or what I did. I had very little ability to see things from another person's perspective. I needed to be right, which would repel people. The reality

> "When we were children, we used to think that when we were grown-up we would no longer be vulnerable. But to grow up is to accept vulnerability. To be alive is to be vulnerable."
>
> – Madeleine L'Engle

was, I couldn't take on new information because it meant I had to be vulnerable – again, stuck in my desperate Wounded Masculine Energy.

I had so much anger and rage trapped inside of me. So much resentment and "white anger", as I used to call it. Suppressed, grabbing onto anything and everything inside me. I felt like it sat in every organ, every limb, and every inch of my hair and body (I believe this is another reason I cut all my hair off.) Anger was something I desperately hid from, but she – because I now call anger a "she," believing it comes from the feminine side of us, not the masculine – always, always wanted to come and say hello, reminding me that she was very much alive and living inside.

The Turning Point: Reconnecting to My Birthright

The turning point in understanding and balancing my Feminine Energy and Masculine Energy came after I fell down the stairs in 2021 and compacted my lower back vertebrae (I told you that story in Book Two: *A New Perspective*). To be honest, I didn't even know much about energy until I started working with Caroline Hales, a renowned Energy Healer on the Mornington Peninsula, Victoria, Australia. She became my mentor – she's a truly special and insightful woman who taught me how to sit with both my Masculine Energy and Feminine Energy, and to feel safe with both.

Initially, we started with anger, because this seemed to be the element I was struggling with the most. She helped me understand anger from a Feminine Energy perspective and how to experience emotions without losing myself. It was through connecting with my Feminine Energy that my life truly began to change for the better.

She helped me understand that anger, though often mischaracterised as purely "masculine" or aggressive, is fundamentally an aspect of unexpressed or repressed Feminine Energy when viewed through a trauma lens.

Caroline taught me that this anger isn't the calm, focused assertiveness of the Healthy Masculine Energy we need for balance. It's often a reflection of the chaotic state of our inner world – a reactive, resentful, and self-sabotaging act, serving only as a desperate, protective shield to create distance from what we're afraid of. Instead, for me, it was a fumbling attempt to demand respect, when the softer Feminine Energy side of me, saying "no", was consistently ignored or invalidated. So, in essence, my anger was my Feminine Energy being disregarded and disrespected. Hence, why I call my anger a "she". Feminine.

So, when unresolved anger rises to the surface, it's really the Feminine Energy within us crying out to be safe, and more importantly, for safe expression – a need to restore our boundaries and balance within ourselves.

Finding Harmony

When I cracked the code on sitting with my anger and feeling safe, I could see its correlation to my Masculine Energy and Feminine Energy. Suddenly, everything became clear. I could see where the Wounded Masculine Energy had taken such a massive stronghold on my life as a "false" protector – my armour. And that, my friend, is where I started to do more work.

Using the core values of challenging, honesty, and acceptance, I went to work dismantling and dissecting my old patterns, determined to find clarity and understand the reasons behind my behaviour.

The control was a big one, and very humbling. Feeling safe allowed me to relinquish this wounded part of myself –and empower me and my Inner Child to change. Vulnerability has become my friend because I no longer feel ashamed of myself. Acceptance helped me resolve that massive hole in my heart. I openly share parts of myself with trusted people, and I don't fall apart. Clearly, I have mastered it if I am able to share all these stories here, too, wouldn't you agree?

If I need space, I ask for it, and that is okay. My time alone is beautiful to me; I never feel lonely, I only feel whole. Why? Because I am in love, I don't need outside validation to tell me I am worthy or lovable; I can do that for myself. Now, I invite my friends into my life when it works for me. I no longer show up to parties where there is an unspoken obligation to attend. I spend my time now doing things and with people who bring me joy, more so, where I choose to share my precious energy.

Listening to my body has become a game-changer. I now treat sleep as a vital gift, relishing these simple, deliberate acts of self-love. The need to be perpetually 'on' has finally vanished. I recognise and appreciate now that my unique strength lies in my capacity for action – my ability to get things done, achieve my goals, and clear my to-do list. I've developed some supreme skills over the years, and my Masculine Energy discipline will always be by my side. I accept that. But then, my Feminine Energy is right there, reminding me to listen to my Inner Voice. As a result, it's now effortless for me to pause, come inside – even when I'm absorbed in my joyous gardening – and tend to my needs. I easily take breaks, hydrate, eat nutritiously, or simply spend time with my beloved fur babies.

I took up painting, and this has become another joy filled space. I even take vacation days simply to paint! I love creating textured art of trees, capturing flickering light and colour. Sometimes I go a bit wild, like when I painted a full-canvas funky chicken in a yoga pose, complete with streams of electric hair. She's awesome. Her name is Betty.

Today, I love feedback. The more the better. I relish hearing how people experience me, what insights they can share. Every day is a school day for me now. Living with a curious lens to the world is incredibly liberating. If I don't agree with someone, based on my values, I don't have to argue the point either – I can nod and allow the other person to be heard. Oh, that feels good; less chaotic exchanges are noticeable. And, oh wow, apologising for my role in something, when I made a misstep or misjudged a situation, now is effortless. I see what I did wrong, I take responsibility for it, and I call it out. People are so accepting of that approach, and there is no shame. It is powerful and comfortable.

There is no ego in Feminine Energy, which I absolutely love. Only lessons. Empowerment through knowledge, and softness through creating space for myself and others to be seen and held safely.

What I've come to appreciate now is that to live in Healthy Feminine Energy means living in harmony with my emotional body, my intuition, and gently, discerningly establishing boundaries. Lovely, healthy boundaries that protect my needs and values. I no longer show up in situations where I feel unsafe or unheard. If someone tries to push past my boundary – I acknowledge what they are doing – and I exit. So, by keeping in my lane, I avoid falling into the same hole as I did in the past. There is no unnecessary pain or self-sacrifice – only situations that arise for me to learn something from and resolve a part of myself that hasn't yet been healed. So, now, when there is a need to feel a raw emotion like anger or rage, I pay attention and work out what it is teaching me.

I found out my Stepmother recently passed – and no one told me. My father's estate disappeared, and no one has been accountable. No information has been forthcoming. Gosh. Horrible. And, yes, it brought up stuff from my past. A huge amount of rage surfaced, huge. However, this time with deep regretful emotion about my relationship with my father.

What was fascinating was how pure the rage felt. How liberating it was to allow that to come up and to be comfortable enough to experience it. When I say "pure," what I mean is that there was no shame attached, no guilt, no "I can't express this" resistance. Only real, compassionate love for Inner Child, and the woman I am today. So, this rage came, reared its ugly head, and then flowed through and out. I acknowledged it. Looked into it and processed it. The messages I could allow myself to hear in this experience were deeply moving – a true sign of liberated transformation. That was my Feminine Energy and Masculine Energy in harmony.

> "Hiding behind high walls, we are safe. But life is not a medieval siege; vulnerability requires a two-way trade. Open the gate and reception is made. Extreme caution leads to emptiness, numbness; Is your life locked away inside a fortress?"
>
> – Virginia Burges

By introducing you to the world of energy, I hope that you can experience what I have. What I found to be my reconnection vessel to a life I now love with all my heart was deeply dependent on my Feminine Energy coming into my life in full swing. I didn't honestly know myself until I plugged into that source. That is the truth. In a way, this whole book, *Liberated Connection*, is based on my own personal experiences with this coming of energetic age within. So, if you find that I'm a little enthusiastic about energy and being connected to your Primal Feminine Energy, it's because I feel like it was the last part of my healing journey that truly brought everything home for me.

> By accepting the Wounded Masculine parts of myself, I finally opened up to connect to the pure beauty of the Feminine Energy. This acceptance was the deep realisation that truly propelled me forward, cementing the confidence and self-trust I stand in today.

10. Connecting to Your Energy

Your Gift to Yourself
A Compassionate Guide to Healing

My friend, I understand what it's like to feel disconnected from yourself, especially when life throws unexpected challenges your way. If you've experienced trauma, you might feel your energy is scattered or blocked, which can be unsettling and leave you feeling uneasy. So, how can we address this? Since this is likely a new skill for you – or perhaps this is a refresher and enhancement of what you already know – I've created a step-by-step guide for you to explore and see how it resonates. My aim is to make this process clear and help you achieve the desired outcome.

Now, like with any new skill, there are instructions. Because connecting to your energy isn't as simple as flipping a light switch, I've broken it down into five segments: creating space for setting intentions, making authentic choices, redirecting relationships, prioritising health, and embracing feminine energy. While these elements are fundamental, I understand they might seem like a lot of work – perhaps even intimidating. It's like a recipe for a fabulous gourmet cake with all the incredible toppings; it takes time and involves a lot of steps to follow. In the same way, it takes effort to make a good, energetic connection within. However, if it feels overwhelming and all you need right now is a little sweetness, not the whole cake, feel free to read through it and focus on just one element to start. You have permission to take it one step at a time. Remember, every small step forward is progress.

Then, in a couple of weeks, revisit this and reread it. Let it sink in. You might not remember every line, but your subconscious will absorb the details, and you may find yourself becoming more curious about energy. Later, when it feels right, you can read it again. Or, you might have already taken photos of these pages on your phone, so you can review them while having coffee, instead of scrolling through social media.

> "Sometimes the smallest step in the right direction ends up being the biggest step of your life."
> – Unknown

I want you to know that you have the ability to learn new skills and create new, life-affirming behaviours. You've already proven you can survive some tough challenges. This shows you are capable of more than you realise. You possess incredible strength, and that special glow of energy and vitality is waiting for you to reach in and connect with it. It's your birthright, and no one can take it away. So, how about I take you by the hand, and we gently explore how you can consciously reconnect with your uniquely colourful energy in those key areas of your life where it can bring far-reaching healing in your Change Experience journey?

Remember, this is a tender exploration and rediscovery of parts of yourself that haven't been acknowledged for a while. Be patient, kind, and gentle with yourself as we navigate these steps together. You are safe here.

Step 1: Creating Your Space and Setting Your Heart's Intention (For All Areas)

This first step gently guides you to create a safe inner and outer space where you can comfortably connect with yourself.

Find Your Place of Calm: Create a quiet, safe space where you feel undisturbed. This could be a cosy corner of your home, a peaceful spot in nature, or anywhere you can have a few precious moments of stillness. Make it yours. It may help to light a candle, bring in a soft blanket, or include anything special to you that makes you feel comforted. Do what works for you. In your style. Your own unique way.

Set Your Intention: Before you start, take a deep, cleansing breath and gently bring your awareness to why you're doing this. What do you truly hope to gain from connecting with your energy right now? Maybe it's clarity around a tough decision, a deeper understanding of a relationship, a greater sense of inner peace, or a stronger bond with your beautiful, resilient, and authentic self. Simply stating your intention, even silently, helps to gather and focus your energy. It's like sending a loving message to your soul.

Ground Yourself with Love: Begin by bringing your awareness to your body. Feel your feet on the ground, your weight supported. You are here, you are present, and you are safe. You can try these light grounding techniques:

- **Deep Belly Breathing:** Inhale slowly through your nose, allowing your belly to rise with each breath. Exhale slowly through your mouth, feeling the light release of any tension or worry. Repeat several times, and with each exhale, imagine letting go of anything that no longer serves you.

- **Body Scan with Kindness:** Slowly bring your attention to different parts of your body, noticing any sensations without judgement. Start with your toes and move upwards, acknowledging each area with love and gratitude. If you find any areas of tension, send them a gentle wave of compassion. (Hopefully, you have already practised body scanning through our work in Book One: *Project Clarity* and Book Two: *A New Perspective*.)

- **Visualisation of Strength:** Take a moment to stand or sit, planting your feet firmly beneath you. Visualise a strong, invisible anchor connecting your feet securely to the ground. Focus on this to quiet the mind and body. Be open to feeling the earth's natural strength rise up, supporting your body. A feeling of stability and calm resilience should arise within.

Step 2: Connecting to Your Energy in Choices (Living Authentically)

This step helps you align your decisions with what simply resonates with your core being, that wise and beautiful part of you that knows your truth.

Remember Your Core Values: Take a moment to reflect on what truly matters to you in life. What values do you need to follow to create new, healthy patterns of behaviour? What principles guide your actions when you feel most authentic and alive? Living with authenticity is your truest beacon; it provides clear, undeniable guidance for your life.

Return to the values work you did in Book One: *Project Clarity* and reflect on your top three values to focus on; notice how they are feeling in your life now. What can you do to reconnect with them today? Or if they are feeling quite good, choose another three to work on, to encourage action in your life.

Bring a Recent Choice to Your Mind: Think about a decision you've recently faced or are currently dealing with, big or small. Gently hold it in your awareness. How did it feel when you arrived at that choice (a clear gut feeling or a conflicted one)? For now, don't worry about how difficult it was to act on the choice (as other factors can influence your energy there). I just want you to focus on the initial message and feeling you experienced when making the tough decision. Sit with that.

Listen to Your Body's Wisdom: As you hold this choice in your awareness, gently bring your attention to your body. Notice any sensations that arise. Does it feel light and open, like a weight has been lifted? Or does it feel heavy and constricted, like a knot in your stomach? Where in your body do you feel this response? Remember, any signals from your body are in absolute truth.

Ask Your Inner Voice for Guidance: Silently ask yourself: "Does this choice honestly align with my value of [mention a specific value]?" Pay attention to the first intuitive feeling or thought that arises. Trust that first spark of knowing and communication you receive. And don't ignore it.

Trust Your Instincts: If a choice feels off or misaligned, trust that feeling. Explore the alternatives that are more compatible with your values. Your inner compass will always guide you towards what is reflective of the authentic you.

Step 3: Connecting to Your Energy in Relationships (Honouring Energetic Boundaries)

This step helps you become more attuned to the energetic dynamics of your interactions and helps you learn to honour your boundaries.

Centre Yourself Before Connecting: Before an interaction, take a moment to centre yourself using the breathwork from Step 1. Set an intention to be present, grounded, and aware of the energetic exchange.

Tune into the Unspoken Language: During the interaction with the person you are setting a new boundary with, pay attention not only to the words being spoken but also to the *unspoken* cues – body language, tone of voice, and the overall feeling you experience in their presence. This will tell you a lot, and you might see things you haven't noticed before.

Notice Your Own Energetic Shifts: How do you feel while interacting with this person? Do you feel energised, uplifted, inspired? Or do you feel drained, tense, or uneasy? Where do you feel these sensations in your body? Your body is your barometer. What is the vibration that this person is holding? Is it high and vibrant, or low and messy?

Trust Your Gut Instinct: Your intuition often communicates through your energy. And this, my friend, is the best truth-telling machine you've got. If someone feels consistently drained or triggers feelings of unease, even if you can't logically explain why, honour that feeling. It's okay to create space and boundaries. This is also your ticket to authenticity.

Reflect and Learn Afterwards: After the interaction, take a moment to reflect on the energetic exchange. What did you learn about the other person's energy and from your own response? What insights did you gain from their reactions to the situation, drama, or narrative that was unfolding between you? (What kind of vibration did it have – high or low?) This awareness will help you make conscious choices about the relationships you nurture moving forward.

Step 4: Connecting to Your Energy for Health (Honouring Your Body's Needs)

This step encourages you to listen deeply to the inner compass of your physical and mental health and will promote balance.

Regular Check-Ins with Yourself: Make it a habit to do regular body scans; first thing in the morning is a good time, and before bed at night (as in Step 1). If you are healing or going through an unsettling period, using this throughout your day is a great help. Notice any areas of tension, discomfort, or ease. This is a great way to let the brain know you are connected, taking care to keep safe and out of danger.

Pay Attention to Subtle Signals: Pay attention to seemingly small signals – a slight headache, a change in appetite, a feeling of restlessness. These can be early indicators of your body's needs.

Ask Your Body What It Needs: In moments of discomfort or unease, pause and silently ask your body: "What do you need right now?" Listen for the intuitive response; perhaps it's rest, hydration, light movement, or a specific type of nourishment. A few validating words, and a reminder that you are safe, can always help too.

Honour Your Needs with Love: Act on the messages you receive from your body. What is it telling you? Prioritise sleep, create simple times to unwind, switch off (rest your mind), eat good food that is right for you, get daily movement, and do simple activities that bring you joy and reduce stress. Remind yourself that you deserve to be cared for, and you are safe.

Recognise The Mind-Body Connection: Observe how your emotions and thoughts impact your physical sensations, and vice versa. (You are now very familiar with becoming friends with your emotions; now this is the next part, to feel the vibrations from them as well.) This awareness helps you understand the interconnectedness of your energy.

Step 5: Connecting to Your Honestly Authentic Feminine Energy (Your Inner Power)

This step invites you to embrace the beautiful qualities of your inner feminine essence, that radiant power that resides within you.

Create Space for Feminine Softness and Nurturing: Intentionally engage in activities that feel light, nurture your feminine energy, and be receptive to it. This could be spending time in nature, listening to calming music, engaging in creative expression, or simply allowing yourself to rest without feeling the need to be productive or "on".

Embrace Vulnerability as Strength: Allow yourself to feel your emotions fully, without judgement or the need to be "strong" all the time. Recognise that vulnerability is a source of deep connection, authenticity, and incredible strength. Stop yourself from saying the words, "I'm fine." Think of what you could replace that with – something that is authentic and true for that vulnerable moment.

Practise Nurturing with Love: Do the things that genuinely nourish your whole being (and your authentic needs). This could be a warm bath, taking your shoes off to feel the grass between your toes, watching an old film that makes you feel good, or a hobby that brings you joy. You decide: what is it that gives you a feeling of being loved?

Listen to Your Intuition, Your Inner Know-How: Like I said earlier, pay close attention to your gut feelings, those subtle nudges of inner knowing. Your truth-telling machine, remember. This helps you build the skill of self-trust, so you can believe that inner voice. It is a powerful aspect of your feminine wisdom.

Cultivate Meaningful Connections: If the goal is for you to be more authentic, then think about seeking the same characteristic in the people you choose to spend time with. Focus on building deeper, more authentic relationships with people who really see and appreciate you, and themselves. Quality over quantity is key here. Nurture those connections with open communication and heartfelt presence.

Believe in Your Capacity for Growth: This is a huge step for building self-trust. Acknowledge your intrinsic worth. Validate and recognise your inner strength and know-how (it really is all there!). Embrace the new and practise what you are learning. Because you do require new skills to deploy the self-empathy, self-compassion, and acceptance that you need to heal. And ... commit to showing up for yourself, every step of the way.

Creating an awareness of your energy is a critical and rather enjoyable life skill. Embrace this work as an ongoing, beautiful dance of self-awareness and self-acceptance. Take your time with this. Be patient with yourself; forgive mistakes, normalise setbacks, and acknowledge every step forward – celebrating your victories and learning from your most significant challenges. Trusting this distinct discernment that resides within you will fundamentally change your life.

Why? Because, as I hope you're now seeing, as you cultivate this connection to your energy in your Change Experience journey, you will begin to find a more natural sense of balance (where there might have been a little chaos before). You will automatically make choices that simply honour your health, moving away from quick fixes and temporary highs. You will consciously navigate relationships and become less tolerant of noise from others, clearly defining what you will and won't accept from people.

You will find that now, with all these new skills, even when it feels a little hard or you get that old friend called fear popping in to say hello, you can wave back and say, "Bye-bye. I'm not available today, thanks, mate." You will be more steadfast. There is

> **"The quieter you become, the more you can hear."**
> – Ram Dass

no going back, no way. It's incredible the clarity with which you see things now. All of this, my dear friend, is how you are effortlessly embracing the primal power and energy within your authentic self. You know, and I know, you are worthy of this feeling and freedom I'm describing here.

You're strong enough. Okay? You <u>can</u> do this Change Experience of healing. You have the capacity. Yes? The day you came into this world, <u>you were</u> worthy of love, and you're <u>just as worthy today</u>, sister. Okay, agreed? Good!

As always, I'm holding your hand.

Traversing Energetic Exchanges

11.
Energetic Loving-Yourself-Actions

Protecting Your Peace
Identifying and Dealing with Energy Hangovers

Ever wake up feeling like you've gone ten rounds with a heavyweight boxer, even though the wildest thing you did the night before was brew chamomile tea, catching up with a friend? You might be experiencing what I like to call an "energy hangover". It's that heavy, sluggish feeling that creeps in, not from one too many vinos but from something just as potent – other people's energy.

Think of energy like air – it's always around us, moving constantly and, yes, passing between us. Just by sitting near someone, you're in their energetic sphere, and their strong emotions, thoughts, and even deeply held beliefs can influence yours. When you spend time with someone who's unloading a heap of trauma, releasing worries, and swimming in negativity, that energy doesn't just disappear into thin air. It finds a new place ... often, in you. It's like being in a room filled with thick, heavy fog – eventually, you're going to feel damp and weighed down. I wonder, does this bring up a familiar feeling for you?

This energetic shift can show up in all sorts of unpleasant ways. You might wake up feeling inexplicably sad, wrapped in a low mood that doesn't seem like your usual self. Maybe you're unusually cross, irritable, snapping at loved ones or your pets for no real reason. For women who've gone through complex trauma or tough life experiences, this can be especially tricky. You might suddenly feel triggered without warning, those old familiar anxieties and fears rising up, making you question yourself, falling back into the old story of "I'm not enough," denying your worthiness, and feeling like the world is that scary, unsafe place you once knew. You could find yourself stuck in the emotional dark tornado that your friend, colleague, partner, or family member unwittingly dragged you into.

Okay, here's the real kicker, my friend – this negative, low vibrational state of energy can pull you so far off your centre, so far from your own values, that you lose sight of what really matters to you. You can get stuck in someone else's negative energetic orbit, feeling powerless to shake it off (enter stage left, the repetitive cycles of unwanted behaviours starting to kick in again). It's like being caught in a sticky web, with each of their negative thoughts and feelings clinging to you, making it harder and harder to remember your own light.

This is why learning how to ground yourself, how to set those vital energetic boundaries, and how to fiercely protect and connect to your own loving energy isn't a luxury – it's *non-negotiable*. Think back to all those incredible skills you cultivated in your Liberation Toolbox: **trusting your authentic instincts** as your compass, your **self-empathy** as your shield, your **powerful breathwork** as your instant cleanser, and your commitment to **acceptance**. These are your allies in safeguarding your precious energy.

> **"I can only please one person a day. Today is not your day. Tomorrow doesn't look good either."**
>
> – Abraham Lincoln

You need to protect that inner sanctuary, that place where you feel connected, safe and grounded, so you can continue to gently work on healing the parts of yourself that still need your loving attention to resolve. Treat this work like your life depends on it, because in a very real way, it does.

Do you hear what I'm saying here, sister? This really is no laughing matter, and I'm sure this has happened to you a gazillion times over. Am I right? It's time to become the fierce and loving guardian of your own beautifully precious energy, yes?

Energy Vampires
Getting to Know Who They Are

Okay, my friend, let's delve into this fascinating and crucial topic – the energy vampire. It's time to shed some light on these individuals who can have such a profound impact on our lives, especially because we are already contending with the complexities of our past trauma, which seems to make us more susceptible to these suckers.

You know, it's funny, we often hear about vampires in movies, but there are metaphoric one's walking walk among us. They're not going to bite your neck – no, nothing that juicy – but they're brilliant at blurring boundaries and draining your emotional energy, leaving you feeling depleted and often not even knowing how it happened.

If you've experienced trauma, you likely possess a beautiful, empathetic spirit. You have a loving, giving nature. It's how you've learned to connect and seek love in return. And, unfortunately, energy vampires have a radar for this. They can sense that you are a beacon of light, a socket they can plug into and take what they want.

When you don't have strong boundaries, you miss the very mechanism that prevents others from draining your energy and scooping out your "good stuff". Most of the time, you might not even notice it's happening until you're left exhausted, empty, miserable, and feeling utterly lifeless.

> Your inner wisdom and your gut are saying,
> "Hand me some proverbial garlic!"

Have you ever wondered why you're always the one giving, the one helping, the one listening, but rarely receiving the same in return? Yes, that's the people-pleaser in you, but, my lovely friend, that's also often the energy vampire at work. Your gentle, soft self wants to help, wants to be there for them. It's your learned behaviour from needing acceptance and giving too much to get love in return. It's also your sweet spot for them, your vulnerable point that can be exploited. Little by little, you wind up in a place where you're solely feeding their needs. Your boundaries blur, your needs become invisible, and then those unwanted behaviours, those destructive coping mechanisms, quick fixes, or automatic behaviours with food and drink, creep back in. You're repeatedly doing something detrimental to your health because the vampire is thinking only of themselves.

> **"When we fail to set boundaries and hold people accountable, we feel used and mistreated."**
> – Brené Brown

I remember a friend of mine who would often say, "Why is everyone always calling me for help? Asking me for this and that and demanding it right now!" She'd complain about how she gave everything but got nothing in return, and she was over it, done and dusted. Well, it was true – she was the giver, and there was tumbleweed on the path when she looked to receive what she'd given out ... she was left with nothing but hollow, one-way friendships.

Question: My friend, have you ever complained that you're feeling this way after spending time with someone? Drained and exhausted? Lacking energy? Like your spirit is withered? Like you don't have enough space or time because you're always helping or giving to someone else?

Perhaps it's time to think about this a little more deeply and see what's really happening with people you invite into your life. Do they fit the bill?

Who Are These People in Your Life?

This is where it gets tricky, right? These energy vampires can be anyone: friends, family members, romantic partners, colleagues, or neighbours. Anyone you have energetic interactions with.

It's often the people closest to you, the ones you're conditioned to care for, that can be the most draining. It's hard to recognise them as energy vampires because, for a long time, they may have been a source of connection or even a source of a twisted form of love.

When you're conditioned to give to get love, these people have been your source, too. When you're conditioned to people-please, to always look out for everyone else's interests before your own, it's hard to separate people-pleasing from being a victim of an energy vampire who is sucking out all your energy.

But think about those moments when you feel low, depleted, and exhausted, with nothing left for yourself. That's when resentment starts to simmer. And in that resentment, the vampire's charm often fades, and the truth begins to become clearer. Before now, you didn't really know what to do about it. And that is okay.

Energy vampires can be incredibly charming, alluring even. They make you feel great while you are running around after them. They're great at making you feel like it's a worthy transaction (because that's, after all, what it is – a transaction). But it's not very good for you at all. It just sends you into another subconscious spiral. It lowers your vibration and opens you up for another trip around the merry-go-round of unwanted behaviours that won't have a good outcome for you. Have you experienced this before?

> **"There are only two kinds of people who can drain your energy: those you love, and those you fear. In both instances, it is you who let them in."**
> – Dr. Albert J. Bernstein

> My friend, in my case, and I suspect in yours, allowing these vampires to spin their web was undoubtedly not living by my values.

So, okay, be brave here, and ask yourself – "Is allowing energy vampires to cross my boundaries in line with my values?" If the answer is "yes", then accept that. But if the answer is "no", what will you do about it?

This won't be easy. It's really hard to confront this behaviour within yourself. I understand. It's a sort of "separation of self"; you need to step outside your automatic, self-critical, self-loathing, "I'm not worthy," traumatised self, and see what she is really doing – with no judgement. This is an inner-relationship-with-yourself issue you need to start seriously thinking about. This is all about making conscious choices.

> **Let's say you value reciprocity (like I do).** The question to ask yourself is, "Does this person give to me on a reciprocal basis?" There needs to be an even exchange of energy. What you give must be given back in equal measure. Effortlessly.

Once you become aware of who these energy vampires are in your life, you can develop your skills (energetic forces) to consciously stand against them, avoid them, or set boundaries to protect yourself. You'll start to feel whole because there is no longer a hole in your energy bucket. You're reconnecting with the energy you possess – in its entirety.

"Love yourself enough to set boundaries. Your time and energy are precious. You get to choose how you use it. You teach people how to treat you by deciding what you will and won't accept."

– Anna Taylor

You're connecting with your role in your relationship with yourself, remember. That's the skill of amazing self-awareness that you are building now. Your radar is becoming more finely tuned, and you'll be able to spot energy vampires a mile away. Eventually, they will stop showing up, as there is nothing for them to suck on. And what is left to do is thank yourself for your beautiful boundaries and self-worth. In this process, the muscle and skills you develop help you get better and better and more confident with setting boundaries, and it will soon become automatic.

Sit with this. Let it wash over you for a while. Later, together, we will work out exactly who they are in your life in some reflection questions. However, it is good to reflect now, while this is at the forefront of your mind, so you allow yourself to see it.

The Creators of Chaos

There's something else you need to be aware of, my friend. Energy vampires often thrive in chaos. Think about it – when someone consistently demands, stirs up drama, and ignores your boundaries, what does that bring into your life? Chaos! And when you find yourself caught up with them or allow them into your life, they can expose you to toxic energy, which is a major cause of ongoing stress. They flourish in this chaos because it keeps the focus squarely on them and their needs. It's also a handy way to deflect from their own internal battles. By stirring up external drama, they avoid dealing with what's going on inside.

Believe it or not, this kind of chaos can become strangely addictive. It's often the underlying reason why people remain tethered to these tumultuous relationships. It keeps you in a state of hyperarousal. It feeds your hypervigilance, which your brain, unfortunately, begins to perceive as normal – it's familiar.

In many cases (though not all), energy vampires carry a lower vibration and seek to siphon energy from others. These individuals will often (but not always) have a negative energetic presence. Negative energies, as we know, breed chaos. And here's the tricky part – the more time you spend with them, the more your own vibration tends to lower itself to match theirs.

Similarly, if you were raised in a chaotic environment, you might unconsciously gravitate towards dynamics and settings that mirror that childhood experience.

Here are some common patterns of chaos

The Emotional Rollercoaster: Their constantly shifting needs and crises can pull you onto a messy emotional rollercoaster, disrupting your inner peace and stability. Energy hangovers are constant.

The Unpredictability: You're left perpetually wondering what demand or crisis will erupt next, keeping you in a state of heightened anxiety and hypervigilance.

Draining Your Resources: It's very time-consuming, this chaotic manipulation of your time; their constant taking depletes what precious time you have available, plus energy, and even financial resources, leaving you feeling stretched thin and deeply resentful.

The Constant Focus on Them, Not You: Their drama and needs become the unwavering centre of attention, pulling focus away from your truest desires, goals, needs, and the simple things that really bring you joy.

The Ultimate Creation of Relationship Strain: The one-sided nature of the relationship creates a sometimes abysmal imbalance and strain, and yet you still feel obligated. This often leads to conflict or to a slow, painful erosion of connection and trust.

Remember This, My Friend: A chaotic life inevitably creates chronic stress and impacts your restful sleep, which fuels more vulnerability for you to be knocked around by your own triggers, leading to the inevitable emotional storms and their consequences. Chaos also invites in all those unwanted automatic behaviours that we have talked about throughout this book series. (This is especially true with quick-fix life choices related to food, alcohol, or drugs.)

> Think for a moment: When you hear the word "chaos", who immediately comes to mind? Take a step back and reflect on this.

Energy Vampires: Their Reasonings
Why Do People Behave Like This?

Understanding why someone who seems like an energy vampire behaves that way is crucial. Honestly, it's been a real game-changer for me in stopping resentment from taking hold. When we understand their motivations, we can create some space between what's happening and our own deep need for love and acceptance.

Let's gently explore the "why" behind their behaviour. It's rarely a conscious, malicious thing, even though it can sting terribly. Peeling back those layers and understanding some of the psychological factors involved can bring clarity, even though it doesn't excuse their actions. Remember, their choices are theirs, not yours. You are absolutely not responsible for them!

Peeling Back the Layers: Why the Constant Taking?

This is the other side of the coin, which often helps with your work on acceptance. Think of an energy vampire as someone with a really deep, often unmet need. It's like their inner well is dry, and they're almost instinctively, maybe even unknowingly, trying to fill it up from those around them. Here are some of the psychological factors that might be at play:

🔍 Lack of Empathy

Often, at the heart of it, there's a struggle with empathy – that ability to simply understand and share someone else's feelings. It's almost as if they don't have the emotional receptors to really feel how their actions affect you. Your feelings just don't seem to register with the same weight as their own. This can come from all sorts of places, like how they were raised or even just their personality. (This can feel very cold on the receiving end, I know.)

🔍 Self-Centeredness (Sometimes Narcissistic Traits)

As we've discussed, there's often a strong focus on themselves. Their world revolves around their needs, desires, and experiences. They might genuinely believe that their problems are bigger, their needs more urgent, and their feelings more important than yours. Occasionally, this can overlap with narcissistic traits, where there's a sense of entitlement and a belief that they're somehow superior, which makes them feel justified in taking what they need without considering the impact on others. (This is what fuels their inner bitterness, so be cautious.)

 Insecurity and Need for Validation

Here's the thing: Sometimes, behind that demanding exterior, there's a deep well of insecurity. By constantly seeking attention, favours, and validation, they might be trying to fill this empty space inside to reassure themselves they're worthy by getting energy and care from others. Your willingness to give becomes like a mirror, reflecting a sense of importance that they find hard to discover on their own. (Sound familiar? This is a very common one.)

 Learned Behaviour and Attachment Issues

Sometimes, these patterns develop very early. If they grew up where their needs were always the priority, or where they learned that demanding attention meant they would get it, these behaviours might have become deeply ingrained. How they formed attachments in childhood can also influence this, leading to a fear of not having their needs met, which causes them to constantly seek reassurance. (This is the stuff they carry around, just like the stuff we are talking about that we carry around.)

 Poor Emotional Regulation

When someone finds it hard to manage their own emotions, they might rely on others to help them. By unloading their anxieties, frustrations, and dramas on you, they seek emotional relief, often without thinking about the burden they're placing on your shoulders. (This is where your energetic hangovers come from.)

 Unmet Needs and Entitlement

There can be this deep feeling of past needs not being met, which leads to a sense of entitlement in their current relationships. They might feel they deserve to have their needs met by others, maybe as a way to make up for what they felt they missed out on before.

> We are all complex, with our own
> relevant stories, aren't we?

Why the Selfishness and Lack of Boundaries?

So, to look at this from a new perspective, that "taking" behaviour really stems from intense self-focus and a lack of genuine empathy. Because they might not truly feel or understand how their actions impact you, and your needs and feelings just aren't a significant part of the equation for them. Their own needs often take centre stage, sometimes to an extreme. Their lack of boundaries usually results from a few connected issues:

🔍 **They Don't Recognise That Others Have Boundaries:** Because their own inner world is so loud, they might not even realise you have your own needs, limits, and energy levels that need to be respected. Your "yes" just becomes another way for their needs to be met.

🔍 **Entitlement Leads to Boundary Blindness:** That feeling of entitlement can make them think they have a right to your time, energy, and resources. Boundaries might feel like an unfair obstacle to getting what they believe they deserve.

🔍 **Exploiting Your Lack of Boundaries:** It's sad, but they often get really good at spotting people who haven't set strong boundaries. Your giving nature, your desire to please, and your difficulty saying "no" can become an open invitation for them to take. It's not always intentional at first, but they quickly figure out who's a reliable source of energy and who won't push back.

🔍 **Their Needs Trump All:** In their mind, their needs are the most important. (This can be explicitly painful if you struggle with a painful past of neglect.) Your boundaries, if they even notice them, are seen as secondary or even irrelevant compared to the urgency of their own needs.

> **"You are the average of the five people you spend the most time with."**
> – Jim Rohn

So, when you first set these new boundaries, be ready for some initial challenges with certain people. A very wise woman told me once, "The only people who get upset when you set boundaries are the ones who benefited from you having none."

> Perhaps you can now recognise that their issue or problem with your boundary stems from them, and not from you. And that, my friend, is incredibly liberating.

A Real Life Story
Meet My Friend, the Energy Vampire

My old friend Sue, she's certainly a treat. She's the kind of woman who turns heads and charms the pants off anyone she meets. All smiles and sweetness – you'd never guess what I'm about to tell you if you met her. This story surrounds a challenging and rather adversarial situation with her partner and colleagues, which appeared deeply unhealthy for all parties involved.

When I would call to say hello, or suggest we go for a walk, our conversations would naturally delve into the ongoing complexities of the relational drama with her partner. She was highly focused on detailing his faults, yet she often treated her own actions as irrelevant or without consequence, which, honestly, made it difficult for me to listen to at times.

She would call regularly, saying it was just to "check in." Then an hour can easily slip by, sometimes more, as I listen, offering soothing words of support and helpful psychological insights, trying to be the steadfast friend she needs. But then the call ends with a swift departure before we can even touch on the happenings in my own world. "Oops, so sorry, must catch up on your news next time!" she'll chirp, or offer a breezy, "You're doing so wonderfully. I just know it!" – compliments that feel more like a polite dismissal than genuine interest. She didn't call to ask how I was at all.

A familiar hollowness would settle in after these calls, a strange depletion of my own energy. That nagging feeling of being used, of our connection being decidedly one-sided, began to take root. And so, I started to build some energetic fences, mild ones at first, recognising the lack of give-and-take. Calls became shorter, sometimes just a quick text exchange. Then came the truth-telling, delivered with my style of pragmatic kindness but without any sugar coating. When she recounted yet another "it was them, not me" complicated life upheaval – this time with her boss – I offered a different lens, a glimpse into the other person's potential experience of her, rather than simply validating her victim narrative.

In this encounter, her boss was upset with her for repeatedly going against their agreed conduct at work. In my estimation, it sounded like Sue had crossed her boss's boundaries on more than one occasion, and she was being told to stop. This was a familiar narrative in our previous conversations; she was proud of doing what she thought was best. Yet her boss had reprimanded her for once again manipulating situations at work for her own gain. From everything she explained to me, it sounded like that was exactly what she was doing – crossing boundaries. I suggested that my friend think about taking responsibility for her role in this situation and consider why her boss may have become angry with her. I encouraged her, gently, to consider that perhaps this might reveal the facts of the scenario. Pointing out that perhaps she could be projecting – triggered from an unresolved wound with her mother. The silence on the other end was palpable. It was clear my shift in approach had landed differently. The call ended abruptly, still with her demanding that her perspective of the scenario prevail.

From there? Radio silence. My messages, my voice notes, went unanswered. Ghosted. It was almost comical. The realisation that our friendship had felt like one ongoing and unpaid coaching session, with me being the designated receptacle for her grief and relationship woes, was very real.

Then, weeks later, I received a text message (more like a text essay), accusing me of siding with her abuser and explaining how that conversation had changed her forever. Her boss was now subject to a case against her for workplace bullying and was labelled an abuser. Gosh – that poor woman. It was also a passive-aggressive F-you, for not telling her what she wanted to hear. To me, her approach felt like a calculated manipulation of words, designed to defend her new narrative of victimhood and deepen a tale of abuse, especially since she had, in fact, lost her job due to her own behaviour. (For the record, at no point did she present the story of her boss as an abuser at the time.)

My response to Sue's message was simply to say, "I won't engage in these types of text messages, and I won't be manipulated."

Her reply was something along the lines of, "Well, then, I guess that will dissolve our friendship." And it did.

The old me would have been simmering with resentment, and then desperately trying to make things right, taking on all the responsibility for this friendship going south. But the new me – the one learning to navigate these currents with a bit more discernment – sees this differently. While a part of me might jokingly think I should have sent her a bill for services rendered, the deeper understanding is that this experience, though initially draining, felt like another soft nudge from the universe. It has ultimately strengthened my boundaries and affirmed my instincts – to truly see people for who they are and to be more conscious of how I show up in these connections. As I have said before, "when someone shows themselves to you, believe them."

> This, I know, is all part of my life's work. I will always have new lessons to learn and continue to face challenging situations that test my resolve. This was certainly one of them. Make no mistake, this stuff is still difficult for me, and I need to be gentle with myself in these sorts of situations.

12. Reflection Time

The Current of Your Connections
Questions Revealing Your Energy Dynamics

Now, my friend, I ask you to take a quiet moment. Really reflect on your own life. Grab your favourite journal, because the insight you're about to uncover is profound.

Every single one of your connections – whether family, friend, or colleague – is fundamentally defined by the way you relate, not simply by the person themselves. Therefore, this exploration isn't about judging specific people; it's about examining the current of energy that flows between you. We're looking for where that current is reciprocal, and where it may be running one way.

These questions are designed to help you honestly identify relationships that may fit the bill on the energy vampire front. But here is the most important lesson, and where the real power lies: as we examine the friction you feel with others, remember that those external irritations often become a powerful mirror showing us precisely where we need to develop within ourselves.

This is your opportunity to move past judgement and into deep self-understanding. This honest reflection provides the necessary awareness to create meaningful, lasting change in your life.

Remember to read your answers aloud to connect to the sensations and awareness of what transpires here.

> Seeing others is intelligence. Seeing yourself within the dynamic of your connections – that is true freedom.

Let's Begin

1. **Who comes to mind?** When you think about the people you spend time with, are there any who consistently leave you feeling a bit ... drained? Perhaps your energy or vitality has been lessened? Take a careful look at your interactions with them. What are those moments genuinely like? What specific things cause you to feel this particular way? Jot down a few names that spring to mind and take a moment to describe what those interactions feel like for you. Be honest, reflective, and specific about the feeling.

2. **What happens when you're around them?** What do you notice about your reactions when you're around them? Do you find yourself acting in certain ways? Are there identifiable patterns in your behaviour? What thoughts or feelings arise when you think about interacting with them? Is there anything that comes up – perhaps dismissive thoughts about your own worth, or a kind of critical self-talk that tends to play on repeat in your mind?

3. **Let's look at different areas.** Now, let's broaden our view a bit. Think about different areas of your life – your professional relationships, your family, your work environment, your hobbies and creative pursuits, and even your spiritual practices (if applicable). Do you notice anyone in those areas who might fit that description? Is there anyone in those areas that takes up a disproportionate amount of your energy? To take this exercise to the next level, you could choose one person from each area that stands out to you and briefly identify why they impact your energy in this way.

4. **Turning the mirror.** This one might take a little courage, so be kind to yourself. Can you think of a time when you might have been the one who left someone else feeling drained? If something comes to mind:

- What was the situation? What was your behaviour like? Describe the dynamics and the circumstances.

- If you could go back to that moment now, what might you choose to do differently?

And, hey, it's totally okay if something comes to mind. Acknowledging this is not a judgement of your character; it simply means we are all works in progress, learning and evolving in our interactions.

Remember, this isn't about judging anyone, including yourself. It's about connecting within – understanding yourself with perspective – and becoming more liberated, aware of the energy flow in your life.

> Use those Liberation Toolbox skills we've talked about: self-trust, acceptance, self-empathy, and self-compassion. This is about empowerment. This is all for your beautiful creation of homegrown, feeling good in your skin, kind of stuff.

...

13.
Don't Give Away Your Power

The D.E.E.R. Technique
Protection From a Permanent Energy Vampire

This is a powerful way to deal with energy vampires, especially those you can't simply walk away from – the people you must interact with due to the structure of your life. Consider this little strategy a valuable tool to keep in your back pocket. I call it the D.E.E.R. strategy.

So, who are these "permanent" energy vampires? They might be colleagues or your boss at work, extended family members you need to stay in touch with, or someone in your community sports group, a volunteer organisation, or even a mothers' group.

I once had a boss who was a master energy vampire – quite diabolical. But I'm grateful to him because he inspired the D.E.E.R. strategy out of necessity. I needed to stay in that job to achieve a particular milestone, and this technique became my protective barrier. I had no choice but to safeguard myself, and thankfully, D.E.E.R. was my sanity and energy saviour. He couldn't rattle me when I used it.

D.E.E.R. is an acronym for **D**on't Get Involved, Don't **E**ngage, Don't Get **E**motional, and Don't **R**espond.

This tool saved me countless hours of pain. I took back control over my rather impulsive and unhealthy behaviours of self-punishment, over my past patterns of mind-numbingly excessive amounts of rich food and a bar full of drinks.

> **"Energy vampires are those people who suck the life out of you by draining your energy and leaving you feeling exhausted."**
>
> – Doreen Virtue

Energy vampires are skilled at throwing metaphorical "balls" into the air, expecting you to catch them. And for the most part, like me, you've probably done just that. You set the expectation that you'd do what they wanted by catching that ball in the first place. From there, it escalated; they ran with the ball, and you followed. They created a situation, and you played along.

When you use the D.E.E.R. strategy, you establish a strong boundary and non-verbally communicate that there will be no "ball catching" today, tomorrow, or any other day. You'll subtly convey that you're no longer participating in that dance, but you'll do it with kindness.

With D.E.E.R., the key is to stay calm, sweet, and seemingly lovely. Mirror their charm and be impeccably gracious, albeit gracious with a firm boundary. What happens is that you disarm the energy vampire. They have no leverage. You're not showing vulnerability, acting out of fear, or seeking their approval. This is a different kind of interaction. You're not reacting to their prompts when they "throw the ball". Your arms aren't outstretched to catch it. Instead, you pivot, turn, and walk away, smiling and wishing them a good day. Ah, bye-bye! It's a beautiful, beautiful way to safeguard your energy.

> Give it a go. See if it works for you. It might take a little practice, but it saved my life for a good year.

D.E.E.R. Technique Outlined

This is your strategy for dealing with those unavoidable energy vampires – a family member, a boss, or a community member who will always be present. Through this process, you'll reduce the toxicity and chaos they create. The four basic principles are:

- **D**on't Get Involved.
- Don't **E**ngage.
- Don't Get **E**motional.
- Don't **R**espond.

1. Don't Get Involved

- When the energy vampire tries to unload their negativity onto you, with your boundary firmly in place, smile and don't react.
- Simply smile.
- Continue to appear happy, and carefree – with your boundary firmly set.

2. Don't Engage

- Instead of absorbing their energy and catching their proverbial ball (performing the tasks you used to get drawn into), just smile and wave. Be amiable, sweet, and lovely, but don't take on their requests.
- Don't do what they want this time. Maintain your smile and your poise. Be incredibly sweet and lovely while standing firm on your boundary.

3. Don't Get Emotional

- You're wise now; you recognise their patterns and can see what's coming.

- You know their words will be unpleasant or intended to provoke you, and you understand this is often a form of gaslighting and a projection of their own issues.

- Knowing this allows you to defuse the situation and uphold your boundary. See their actions/words/conversation for what they are, and don't respond with emotion.

- Detach any personal meaning from their actions and maintain your boundaries.

4. Don't Respond

- Your boundary skills are your greatest asset here!

- Don't offer any reaction to their bait, their words, or their attempt to provoke you. Be easy-going. Just offer a smile.

- If needed, you can simply say, "Okay" or "Interesting."

- An excellent technique is to deflect by commenting on something neutral and monotone, like the weather, an object nearby, the next meal, or your next activity.

- Maintain your smile and keep your vibration and energy high and grounded.

After Practising This Technique

After implementing and playing out your new skill with the D.E.E.R. technique a few times, I'd like you to observe yourself and take some time to reflect:

- Notice what happens to your energy levels.

- Notice what happens to your emotions. Do they affect you as much?

- Notice what happens to your confidence.

- Notice what choices you feel you have in the situation now.

- Notice how others begin to interact with you as they observe your boundaries.

> "Don't let the behaviour of others destroy your inner peace."
> – Dalai Lama

It might feel awkward at first, which is natural for anything new, but that's perfectly okay. With practice, it becomes easier and feels more natural. And remember, practising the D.E.E.R. technique is all about reinforcing the self-protection that leads to greater inner peace.

From here, I want you to sit with this. This is another step closer to more awareness. Observe what you notice in your relationships, friendships, work, or how you show up. Acknowledge that you are a wise woman, taking your time to flourish.

> Please remember to give yourself some warm validation. Tell yourself you are a beautiful woman with many layers, colours, and experiences that have taught you a great deal.

14. My Trauma Experience

Know-How to the Rescue
Taking Back My Power with D.E.E.R.

There is a common theme in past trauma stories, and it is one that I share. My journey has been profoundly shaped by wounds inflicted by those who should have been my protectors. As I stepped into the professional world, I longed for a different dynamic, one of growth and mutual respect. Instead, I encountered a male boss whose behaviour cut me to the core. It wasn't merely challenging; it felt like a relentless emotional assault. He was the very definition of an energy vampire, each interaction leaving me utterly drained, as if my life force was slowly being siphoned away. This mirrored the unsafe and unpredictable environments of my past, instantly triggering a familiar state of hypervigilance and anxiety.

In the demanding landscape of my career in Asia, I found myself reporting to a man whose initial charm masked a deeply troubling nature. What began as seemingly innocuous professional interactions gradually morphed into something unsettling. The ping of after-hours selfies on my phone was the first jarring note, a clear signal that boundaries were being crossed, and I was venturing into precarious territory. This marked the beginning of a distressing chapter, where my workplace, a space meant for collaboration and achievement, became the arena for an insidious abuse of power.

As I navigated this challenging professional relationship, the subtle shifts in his behaviour escalated into blatant disrespect. During meetings, his hand would linger a moment too long on my leg, a violation that sent a shiver of unease through me. His "jokes", like suggesting I do "nudie runs" as a reward, were crude and demeaning, stripping away my sense of professionalism and comfort. The late-night calls, accompanied by more unsolicited selfies and requests for personal pictures, felt like a constant invasion of my privacy. He peppered his language with overly familiar and objectifying terms – "darling", "gorgeous", "sweetie", "my lovely" – especially in front of clients, reducing me to a mere object of his gaze and commentary. Each instance chipped away at my confidence, leaving me feeling sexualised, deeply compromised, and deeply uncomfortable in my own skin.

Despite the discomfort I felt, and because of the violation, I knew I had to draw a line. Rejecting his inappropriate advances and reporting his behaviour to HR felt like a necessary step to reclaim my personal and professional boundaries. However, this act of self-assertion seemed to ignite a darker side of him. His friendly facade crumbled away, replaced by a palpable toxicity and cruel manipulation. It felt like a direct punishment for not complying with his desires, for refusing to indulge his inappropriate needs any longer. The consequences were swift and painful, leaving me to navigate a hostile work environment where I felt increasingly isolated and forced to endure his retaliatory behaviour.

His constant inappropriate behaviour, the sexualisation, the undermining – it was like living near a volatile volcano, with each interaction acting as a trigger that sent tremors through my already fragile emotional landscape. Behind the professional mask I had to wear, I was unravelling. The isolation and confusion he fostered, so reminiscent of past betrayals of trust, drove me to seek solace in destructive patterns. The need to numb the pain became overwhelming, leading to nights fuelled by alcohol and cigarettes. Large amounts of Asian food became a temporary comfort, a way to fill the emptiness his actions created (I would order enough for a family, justifying it because I wanted more flavours to try!). These unhealthy coping mechanisms, hidden from my professional world, were the desperate cries of someone trying to survive the toxic fallout of his abuse of power, a stark contrast to the composed facade I had to maintain each day.

Compounding this was the insidious voice of my past trauma, the ingrained belief that "I am not good enough." This narrative had me trapped, pushing myself to endure his draining behaviour, desperately trying to prove my worth and silence that inner critic. I laboured under the illusion that by tolerating more pain, I could somehow prove I was capable and deserving. This only made me more susceptible to the constant emotional drain of his abusive and energy-sapping approach. I felt stuck, caught in a torturous loop of wanting to succeed professionally while battling the deep-seated feeling of inadequacy his actions amplified.

> **"You can't control what happens to you, but you can control your response to it."**
> – W. Clement Stone

Discovering the D.E.E.R. strategy – **D**on't Get Involved, Don't **E**ngage, Don't Get **E**motional, and Don't **R**espond – felt like grasping a sturdy branch in a raging river. It wasn't a quick fix, but it provided a concrete framework for navigating the toxic interactions that threatened to overwhelm me. By consciously implementing these principles, I began to create a much-needed boundary, a protective layer against the constant barrage of negativity that had been leaching my energy and reinforcing old wounds.

Each time my boss attempted to draw me into conflict, to bait me with criticism or unreasonable demands, I consciously chose a different path. I would offer a polite smile, remain outwardly calm, and refuse to take the bait. It was an active choice not to get emotionally entangled, not to allow his negativity to penetrate my carefully constructed defences. Slowly, subtly, the dynamic began to shift. I wasn't fuelling his energy vampire tendencies with my reactions. The hypervigilance that had been my constant companion started to quiet, replaced by a sense of growing inner control.

This deliberate act of non-engagement was deeply liberating. It created a space where I could observe his behaviour without being consumed by it. The relentless internal battle against feeling "not good enough" began to ease as I stopped internalising his negativity. I started to recognise my own competence, my skills, separate from his distorted perception. It wasn't about changing him; it was about reclaiming my power, my sense of self-worth. The D.E.E.R. strategy wasn't just a tool for managing a difficult boss; it became a catalyst for healing, for stepping out of the shadows of past abuse and into a place of greater self-respect and dignity. It cleared the path for me to breathe again, to experience moments of genuine peace, and to move forward with the unwavering knowledge that my worth is inherent and unshakeable.

> And in the end, as these things often play out, his behaviour became his undoing. The consequences he sowed were his to reap. Let's just say, the universe has a way of balancing the scales, and in this instance, justice, in its own time, was indeed served. (They finally fired him!)

The Liberating Power of Boundaries

15.
The Boundary Blueprint

Designing Your Life on Your Terms
Unpacking the Art of Healthy Boundaries

In these following pages, I really want to share why boundaries are so essential for becoming a liberated woman. Truly, they're a gift, a constant source of peace, joy, and that real, deep-down happiness we all crave. Think of them as a safe, loving space for yourself, where you can make choices that feel right. Because when you have those boundaries in place, the old triggers that used to send you spiralling into unwanted behaviours don't have the same power anymore. And, bringing it back to the heart of this journey, boundaries are generously here to help you reclaim your power and heal your relationship with food and alcohol, too.

Setting a healthy boundary means gently, but firmly, separating your energy, your emotions, and your thoughts from everyone else's. It's about creating a clear, loving space around your own precious self and honouring that space consistently. There are so many kinds of boundaries to discover that you need in your life, and honestly, this is one of those must-have skills that can change everything. To get you started, to help you see where these apply in your own life, let's explore four key areas together.

- **Emotional:** Protecting your emotional balance and giving you the ability to freely connect to your emotions (and not avoid them).

- **Physical:** Protecting your personal physical space.
- **Sexual:** Protecting your needs and safety sexually.
- **Workplace:** Safeguarding your ability to work without interference or drama.

For Many of You: Boundaries Possibly Didn't Exist

Growing up, so many of us were taught to bend over backwards, to twist ourselves into knots, just to make sure everyone else was comfortable. Our parents, bless their hearts, never even used the word "boundary". It just wasn't part of their world, or vocabulary, and not something they were raised with as a value. Back then, self-sacrifice was seen as this noble, almost holy thing – like it made you a better person. It was the overarching value. But what we realise now, and what I had to learn the hard way, is that all that "self-sacrifice" really meant was that we didn't have any boundaries. None. We didn't know how to ask for help, how to take care of our own needs, or even what those needs *were*. And honestly? That's not how you build a rich, meaningful, fulfilling life.

You know, it's funny, the whole idea of personal boundaries has really taken off since the mid-1980s, but now feels like a buzzword, or a throw-away line, like a dog with a bark but no bite. But I wonder how many people really know how to set a boundary or use them effectively in their lives? Maybe that's why so many self-help books and support groups have brought it into the light! Because at its heart, it's simply about speaking your truth, and that is what so many people struggle to do.

> **"Daring to set boundaries is about having the courage to love ourselves, even when we risk disappointing others."**
> – Unknown

Really, setting boundaries is all about clearly stating what you stand for, so that those precious values of yours don't get trampled on. And let me tell you, my friend, learning to set and hold those boundaries? It's like unlocking a superpower for healthy relationships. It's the secret sauce for building real trust and connection with yourself, and other people. Sure, some folks might get a bit ruffled when you start drawing your lines in the sand, but deep down, they'll respect you for having the courage to stand tall for what you believe in. Or they will walk away – in which case, let them. Trust me on this one.

Okay, if you are not up for more "how to" unpacking, and don't have the headspace for deep skill building, or don't want to get into the nitty gritty, all good. I've got you covered. Here are three quick tips on how to implement boundaries until you are ready.

Three Easy Steps to Setting Healthy Boundaries:

1. Be clear and straightforward. Speak calmly and avoid raising your voice.
2. State your needs or requests directly. Focus on what you want rather than what you don't want.
3. Acknowledge and accept any discomfort that arises. This might include guilt, shame, or remorse, which is common for people with poor boundaries, co-dependency issues, or those who tend to be people pleasers.

Three steps, is that all? Sorry, no. You know this is not the book about quick fixes, is it? So, let's carry on, shall we? Let's continue to work on building the skills and the layers, so you can get this right, and hold onto those skills with some gusto! (That's what I want for you!)

The "Why"
Why Learning to Set Boundaries Matters So Much

Alright, let's talk about *why* all this boundary stuff is so incredibly important. To guide you through this process, I want to share some helpful principles – the kind that have really stuck with me and made a difference in my own life. Think of these as your foundation, your go-to reminders as you start building and strengthening your boundaries.

Things to Remember When Setting Boundaries

🔗 **Your Health**: It's simply *your* responsibility, yes? That's not something to feel stressed about – it's something to embrace! You are 100%, without a doubt, responsible for your own health, your own happiness, and that beautiful sense of balance in your life. And you know what? That's not selfish at all. It's essential. It means gently, and initially, bravely putting your own needs first. Not in a demanding way, but in a way that shows yourself the same respect and care you so freely give to others. When all your precious energy is constantly flowing outwards, into everyone else's needs, you end up running on empty. And when you're running on empty, my darling friend, it's almost impossible to really care for yourself. It leaves you feeling weak, vulnerable, and disconnected. What's more, when you're in that state, it becomes so much harder to even *hear* your own needs, let alone address them effectively. That's where boundaries come in. Implementing a loving boundary, wherever you need it in your life, creates a solid, unshakable foundation of "loving yourself activities". It's like giving yourself a big, warm hug and saying, "I've got you. I'm here for you."

🔗 **Boundaries Let You Thrive:** When you put those beautiful, healthy boundaries in place, you don't just survive, my friend. You *flourish*. It's like finally giving yourself permission to take a deep, cleansing breath. And listen, when you let people casually step all over your boundaries, there's always a cost. Always. And trust me, it's *you* who ends up paying that price if you don't address it. It might show up as resentment, that heavy weight of exhaustion, or just a deep, unsettling feeling of being unfulfilled. (Nope, not worth putting yourself through all that again, right?)

- **Own Your Emotions:** We know this now, don't we? *You are* responsible for your own emotions – every single one of them. You need to acknowledge them, really *feel* them, and hold them within your own precious emotional space. You're also responsible for expressing those feelings in a healthy way. Clearly and simply stating your expectations and needs in any relationship. This clarity, this new perspective and honesty with yourself and others? It's a total game-changer. It's what helps you set those boundaries with purpose and ensures you're getting what you need and want out of this beautiful, precious life.

- **No Guilt Allowed:** There is absolutely, positively no guilt involved in having boundaries. None. Zilch. Zero. Having boundaries simply means learning to say "no" sometimes. And you know what? You don't need to over-explain or apologise for it. Without those healthy boundaries, you're at risk of slipping into those old co-dependency patterns, and, my darling friend, that road leads straight to burnout. I've been there, and trust me, it's not a place you want to be.

- **Deal Directly and Honestly:** You are responsible for addressing any issues directly with the person involved. Be honest with yourself and be honest with them. Share your experiences openly, from the heart, and absolutely decline to do anything you don't want to do. It's your life, your choice. You are in the driver's seat.

- **Respond in the Moment:** The best way to keep those boundaries strong and robust is to respond in the moment. Don't let things fester, my friend. Clarify your expectations right then and there, rather than just quietly accepting what someone else wants. It might feel a little awkward at first, but I promise you, it gets easier with practice. You'll find your voice, and it will become your superpower.

Remember, setting boundaries takes practice, just like anything else. But I promise you, the more you do it, the better you'll become at it, and the more freedom and peace you'll find in your everyday life!

The "How"
Unlocking the Secrets to Setting Solid Boundaries

Alright, my friend, let's get down to the nitty-gritty of how we make these boundaries happen. To positively master the art of setting healthy boundaries – and believe me, it is an art – there are some key factors I want to share with you. These aren't just some dry, theoretical concepts; they're the real, practical tools that have completely transformed my own journey, and I know, deep down, they can help you too.

 ## Living By Your Values

Let's say this together, 1, 2, 3... "When I'm crystal clear about what genuinely matters to me, my boundaries help me to live by my values."

I hope that message is clear now. It's your own incredible internal anchor, there so you're not tossed around by the whims of others or constantly second-guessing yourself, wondering if it's "okay" to prioritise your own needs. Once you've taken the time to identify those values, setting and sticking to your boundaries becomes much easier, almost instinctive. Take a moment to think about the person you honestly want to be, both now and in the future. Let those dreams, those aspirations, guide the boundaries you need to establish.

 ## Having Self-Awareness

Boundaries are, at their heart, all about creating safety and trust in your relationships – and that starts with the most important relationship of all: the one you have with yourself. Self-awareness is key here. You need to really know your own expectations, your own discomforts, and those situations that just drain your energy or inflame those old wounds. Remember when we talked earlier about recognising your role in energy exchanges? That applies here, big time. Start paying close attention to your body language, your gut feelings, and the messages they're sending you.

You always, always have the power to choose how you show up, how you share or protect your precious energy.

🔗 Clear Communication

Setting a boundary isn't a silent act; it's about open, honest, and, yes, a little bit brave communication. It's not enough to simply think, "Okay, this is my boundary now." You need to express it clearly and specifically to the people in your life.

When you decide to set a boundary, try to communicate it in a clear and simple way. You really don't need to over-explain or apologise excessively. A simple, "Thank you so much for the offer, but I won't be able to do that," or "I need to finish what I'm working on right now, I'd prefer to chat later," is often more than enough.

And remember, being direct is absolutely not the same as being unkind. You can be warm, respectful, and still stand firmly in your truth, stating your needs clearly. Think of it as being honest and honouring yourself.

I know it might feel a bit awkward or clunky at first, and that's perfectly okay. Sometimes, people in your life who are used to you not having boundaries might try to keep crossing your new ones. So, you might need to be very literal, very clear: "Here is my boundary – and this is exactly what it means – and I need you to respect it."

With practice, you'll find your own rhythm, your own way of doing things, and you'll learn to communicate your boundaries with both assertiveness and grace. And don't forget, non-verbal cues matter just as much! Your body language, facial expressions, and gestures all contribute to the message you're sending.

🔗 Having Assertiveness

Assertiveness is all about expressing your feelings openly and respectfully. It's not about making demands, but it is about making sure you're heard and understood. Setting healthy boundaries requires you to assert your own needs and priorities as a form of loving yourself (my way of saying self-care). This might feel like a brand-new skill for you – it certainly was for me! It's about finding the strength to say, "I'm not available right now," or "I can't accept that" (and if you feel comfortable, you can add "because it goes against my values"). As you become more assertive, you'll be able to hold your ground without wavering or being swayed by pressure.

Your boundaries are your sacred lines, protecting your peace, your energy, from imbalance and chaos. Be prepared, though. When you start setting boundaries, some people will test them. They might try to push past them because they're used to getting their way. Just observe how they react. It might feel uncomfortable, but it's a valuable lesson. Trust me on this; you will be tested. But always remember, you are ultimately responsible for how you allow people to treat you. You're not a child anymore; you have the power to choose.

It's Okay to Say "No"

This can be a tough one, especially if you're used to being a "yes" person or feeling overly responsible for other people's feelings. But "no" is a complete sentence. It's a powerful affirmation of your own needs and limits.

Remember this: You don't always need a reason. "No, thank you," is perfectly acceptable. If you feel the need to explain, keep it brief and focused on your own capacity, not on judging the other person's request.

Prepare for Different Reactions

People who aren't used to your boundaries might react in all sorts of ways. Some might be understanding; others might be confused, disappointed, or even push back quite strongly. This isn't a reflection of your worth or the validity of your boundary; it's often about their own comfort zones and expectations. (Just know that not everyone will be pleased with your new boundaries, and that is okay.)

Have a few special, ready-to-go responses prepared for potential pushback, like, "I completely understand you're disappointed, but this is what I need," or "I'm not able to discuss this further right now."

🔗 Be Consistent (But Also Flexible with Yourself)

Consistency really helps others understand and respect your boundaries over time. However, please, please be gentle with yourself. There will be times when you feel unsure or when upholding a boundary feels particularly challenging.

It's okay to reassess and adjust your boundaries as you grow and as your circumstances change. The whole goal here is to find what feels healthy and sustainable for you.

My friend, remember that setting boundaries is not selfish; it's essential for your process to get unstuck. It's about honouring your own precious energy and fostering relationships based on mutual respect. You are so worthy of having your needs met and learning to set these boundaries is a powerful way to reclaim your sense of self and build a more peaceful and authentic life.

> Be patient and kind to yourself throughout this process.

The Costs
The Consequences of Not Holding Your Boundaries

As you and I have now explored throughout this book series – together as women who've navigated the fires of life's colourful challenges and complex trauma – we need to have an honest chat about what happens when we don't build those vital walls of protection, those boundaries.

It's not about being difficult or unloving; it's about finally claiming the raw and real inner peace and home-grown joy we so deeply deserve.

> "When we fail to set boundaries and hold people accountable, we feel used and mistreated. This is why we resent people we love and become angry with people we respect."
>
> — Lysa TerKeurst

Think about it for a moment. When someone repeatedly disregards your needs, your time, your physical space, or your emotions, what stirs within you? That familiar knot of anxiety might tighten in your stomach. The weariness that seems to cling to you might deepen. The quiet voice inside that's whispering, "This isn't right", might grow louder, eventually becoming a shout of resentment.

The Cost of Not Having Boundaries

Without boundaries, my friend, we become like open fields with no fences. Anyone can wander in, take what they want, and leave us feeling depleted and used. For someone who has already experienced trauma, this lack of protection can have profound consequences.

- 🔍 **Re-Traumatisation:** When our boundaries are constantly crossed, it can echo past experiences of violation and powerlessness, triggering old wounds and re-traumatising us emotionally and even physically.

- 🔍 **Erosion of Self-Worth:** Repeatedly having our needs ignored sends a damaging message: that our needs don't matter. This chips away at our self-esteem and reinforces the harmful beliefs that might have taken root during our difficult past.

- 🔍 **Increased Anxiety and Fear:** Living without boundaries means constantly anticipating potential intrusions and disrespect. This keeps our nervous system on high alert, fuelling chronic anxiety, hyper-vigilance, and a deep-seated feeling of unsafety.

🔍 **Burnout and Exhaustion:** Always giving, always accommodating, always putting others first – without boundaries, this becomes our default. It leads to emotional, mental, and physical exhaustion, leaving little room for joy or even basic loving-yourself-actions.

🔍 **Strained and Unhealthy Relationships:** Relationships without clear boundaries become breeding grounds for resentment, manipulation, and co-dependency. We might find ourselves surrounded by people who take advantage of our giving nature, rather than offering genuine connection and respect.

🔍 **Suppressed Anger and Resentment:** When our boundaries are crossed, anger is a natural response. But if we don't have the tools to express or act on that anger in a healthy way, it can turn inward, leading to resentment, bitterness, and even physical ailments.

🔍 **Loss of Authenticity:** Trying to please everyone and avoid conflict by not setting boundaries means we lose touch with our true selves, our values, and our desires. We become a reflection of others' expectations rather than living authentically.

🔍 **Hindrance to Healing:** True healing from trauma requires a sense of safety and control. Without boundaries, we remain vulnerable, making it harder to process past pain and move towards a peaceful future.

> How does it feel for you when someone dismisses your feelings, ignores your requests, or invades your personal space? Does it feel disrespectful? Can it make you feel small, unheard, and even angry? Does it erode your trust and damage the foundation of the relationship?

What Happens When a Boundary Is Crossed?
What I Need and Want from a Boundary

I want to share what having a boundary means for me personally. I am incredibly protective of my boundaries now; I feel like a lioness. There is no scary growl or roar, just a quiet presence, a deep knowing, and a confident clarity. This is truly incredible, coming from someone who was raised with absolutely no boundaries, living dangerously without them until I was roughly forty-seven years old. But now, my friend – oh yes, my boundaries are firmly in place. Don't cross them. Thank you very much!

In the first place, though, I am very clear now on what my boundaries are. I can't get upset if someone crosses a boundary that I haven't communicated or made known. This is my role and my responsibility in my life; I have to be diligent in this space, otherwise, chaos can creep back in.

Once my boundaries are in place, for me, when a boundary is crossed, it feels like a genuine violation. It signals immediately that my needs are not being valued. This lack of respect instantly creates a new distance between me and that person. Therefore, the clear consequence of crossing my boundary will be a necessary evaluation of how much of a shift needs to happen in our relationship.

> **"The more you value yourself, the healthier your boundaries are."**
> – Lorraine Nilon

If this resonates with you at all, then that is a positive discovery. What I require from a boundary is profound respect for my needs and for my physical and emotional stability. I want to feel safe and secure in all my interactions, and to conserve my energy for the people and pursuits that genuinely nourish me. My goal is to build connections based on mutual care, reciprocity, and consideration. Ultimately, I want to create a life filled with authenticity, peace, and joy, and boundaries are vital tools to help me achieve that.

I recognise now that setting and maintaining my boundaries is my liberated love language to myself – it is all about trust, compassion, and acceptance. It is about finally saying, "My emotional health matters, and I will protect it." The truth is, once I experienced a consistent level of peace and joy, there was no turning back. I just couldn't go back to chaos; not a chance. My world has shifted far too much to even consider a life without boundaries, even though maintaining them can be a challenge at times.

Okay, so, here are some deeper insights into what goes through my head when someone crosses my boundaries. Honestly, it is never easy, but through careful consideration and action, I manage to keep myself upright. Let me share some of my inner dialogue. If it helps you, please give yourself permission to do the same.

Here's a glimpse into my inner dialogue when someone crosses my boundary

I may want to create distance: I feel this sudden urge to pull back, you know? Like I need to create some space, just for me, to protect my energy. It might mean talking less, keeping conversations shorter, or maybe even needing to step away from the relationship for a little while. I need to breathe and bring my energy back to being grounded.

I know I need to stop oversharing and limit information: A little voice inside says, "Okay, be careful." I might start holding back, sharing less of myself. If I feel like my vulnerability has been taken for granted or used against me, I get protective of my heart. I don't want to expose it again if it's just going to get hurt. And my gut is loudly saying, "Stop what you are doing!"

I may choose to alter the nature of the relationship: If it keeps happening, if a specific boundary keeps getting pushed, I might feel like the relationship needs to shift. It's sad, but sometimes if I become more formal with the person, distance is created. This naturally detaches from the presumption of "being close means you can cross my boundary". It's not that I don't care; it's just that I need to protect my emotional wellbeing. I need to feel safe.

It must be pragmatic: I may need to make a call. Honestly? If it's consistent and my safety or emotional balance are seriously affected, I might have to make the toughest decision of all.

I might need to walk away for good. It's not about punishing anyone or screaming out for validation from that person, either. It's about me. It's about looking after myself, creating a life where I feel safe, respected, and where I can truly thrive. Because, my friend, as I said, this is such a perfect saying, "Believe someone when they show themselves to you." Their behaviour isn't going to change. So, knowing that, it must become all about honouring my own self-trust and my own worth.

Looking after the woman I am today: This isn't about "I'm not enough" or "Why is this happening to me?" inner dialogue. Goodness no. That's the punishment my Former Self would dish out. No more of that, sister; this is all about self-preservation. It's about creating an environment where I feel safe, respected, and able to thrive. Acceptance. You see that magnificent thing come into play again. Accepting what I need and who I am helps me hold on to that self-preservation.

Hold the line, sister. It's worth it.

What's Up Next ...

Alright, sister, let's step out of the shadows and into the light, shall we? I want to take you somewhere dear to my heart now, a place I found quite challenging for a while, I will admit, but then incredibly freeing once I understood why I was working through this. I'd like to gently share some new insights about taking responsibility for yourself, in a bid to help you move out of keeping your shadow attachments locked away (a trap for low vibrational energy to get stuck, dragging you down). I hope you'll work with me on this. I'll ask you to be brave and trust me. Sometimes, facing ourselves can be tough, but it's worth getting to know these parts of who we are.

With willingness, compassion, and complete honesty, you can create another meaningful shift. It's a bit like stepping into a sunlit clearing after a long walk in the cold, lonely shadows.

The Light and Dark in All of Us

16.
I'm Fine

Unveiling the Truth Beneath the Smile
Finding Liberation in Your Full Story

We've all seen her, haven't we? Maybe, if we're raw and honest, we *are* her sometimes. The woman who seems to carry the weight of the world on her shoulders, yet when asked, offers that tight smile and a quick, "Oh, I'm fine, really." She's the one who's weathered storms that would break most of us, the one who's faced down darkness and somehow kept going. And the world often applauds her resilience, her stoicism. "She's so strong," they say. "Never complains." But what if that outer strength is a carefully constructed fortress, built brick by painful brick, to keep the world – and even herself – from seeing the cracks within?

For so many of us who've navigated the jagged edges of unmet childhood needs, the deep ache of neglect, the lingering wounds of adverse experiences, or the shattering impact of adult trauma, denial can become a well-worn cloak. When the pain feels too immense, too raw, our mind, in a desperate attempt to protect us, builds walls. We might find ourselves denying the persistent ache of a past that wasn't safe or denying the way those early experiences continue to shape our present.

And sometimes, that denial manifests in ways that seem to offer solace but ultimately deepen the shadows. The comfort we seek in food, the temporary escape in alcohol, the numbing lull of addiction – these can become ways we deny the very pain they're meant to soothe, creating a vicious cycle that keeps us further from our true selves.

> **"What we deny, we can't heal. What we suppress, we empower."**
>
> – David Richo

Think about it, my friend. Have you ever found yourself drawn back to the very person who caused you such grief? Maybe it's a parent who consistently let you down, or a past partner who inflicted pain. It can be baffling, this pull. But often, it's rooted in a deep denial of our own worthiness, a desperate clinging to the hope that *this time* will be different, that *this time* we'll finally receive the love and acceptance we so deeply crave. We might deny the repetitive patterns in our lives – the overeating that leaves us feeling physically and emotionally heavy, the extra glass of wine, chocolate, or whatever dulls the edges but steals our clarity. We might even find ourselves accepting poor behaviour from loved ones or partners, minimising their actions, because the thought of facing the truth – that we deserve better – feels too terrifying.

And then there's the insidious nature of abuse, the gaslighting and manipulation that can leave us questioning our own reality. We might deny the red flags, the gut feelings that scream "Danger! Run!" because the alternative – acknowledging that someone we care about is intentionally hurting us – is too unbearable. It's a twisted kind of acceptance, a denial of our own intuition in the desperate hope of feeling loved, of belonging.

Perhaps the deepest layer of denial comes from the fear of being alone, the echo of past traumas that whisper, "You are weak. You are helpless." So, we put on a brave face. We become the "resilient one", the "rock solid" woman who's "perfectly fine". We construct this elaborate outer mask, this false self, to navigate the world, all the while carefully guarding the vulnerable, hurting woman within. This stoicism, this refusal to complain, is often mistaken for strength. But beneath the surface, it's a denial of our authentic selves, a denial of the very real pain that's festering inside.

"Why do we do this?" you ask. Often, it's about survival. When vulnerability felt dangerous in the past, we learned to shut down, to become self-sufficient in our pain. It can also be deeply rooted in shame – the heavy, suffocating feeling that there's something inherently wrong with us, that our experiences have somehow made us less worthy of love and connection. This shame makes it easier to hide, to deny, than to face the possibility of judgement or rejection.

But here's the truth, sister: Being in denial is like wading through thick mud. It keeps you stuck, mired in old patterns, and it casts a heavy shadow over your radiant energy. It lowers your vibration, making you more susceptible to physical ailments, emotional pain, and an overwhelming sense of isolation. That bright, vibrant energy that is your birthright becomes clouded, dimmed by the weight of all that you're trying to suppress.

The path towards true healing, towards connection to your feminine energetic power and joy, can leap forward with a delicate act of courage – the willingness to peek behind the curtain of denial. It's about being open to becoming friends with your shadows, those parts of yourself you've tried so hard to hide. They hold stories, yes, and some of those stories might be painful. But within those shadows also lie know-how, resilience, and an incredible capacity for growth.

Imagine the energy that could flow freely within you if you released the need to maintain that facade and heavy cloak of "I'm fine." Imagine the lightness that would fill your world if you allowed yourself to be truly seen, truly felt. It won't be easy, this journey of gentle unveiling. Sorry, I can't promise everything is going to be rosy. But I do promise you, on the other side of denial is a different capacity to feel. A more authentic self, a more raw and honest you. Oh, to experience your own true energy and watch how you start to see the world differently. To evolve and change. To have more capacity for home-grown peace and joy. What a winning ticket that will be.

> Be brave, my friend. You are so worthy
> of stepping back into the light.

 ## Making Friends with Your Shadows

There are parts of ourselves that we often keep locked away in the deepest corners of our being, shrouded in shame and regret. These are our shadows – the aspects we'd rather not acknowledge, the times we've acted in ways that don't align with the woman we truly want to be. Especially after experiencing trauma, these shadows can grow long and menacing – fuelled by reactions to triggers, desperate attempts to avoid overwhelming emotions, and the lingering echoes of past pain.

Can you create a safe space to allow yourself to think about those moments, my friend? The times when a sudden trigger pulled you under, leading you to react in ways that left you feeling hollow and ashamed. Perhaps it was a sharp word flung in anger, a boundary crossed that you later regretted, or a choice made in a haze of trying to numb an unbearable feeling. This discomfort may have manifested in regrettable behaviours – seeking a fleeting high or escape through too much of a chosen substance. This was often a desperate attempt to feel anything different, which ultimately resulted in feeling empty, shamed, or even foolish.

And for some of you – and my heart aches to even touch upon this – there may be a deeper, more unfathomable shadow. The memory of a night when you had too much to drink and found yourself in a compromised situation with someone unsafe, a man who took advantage of your vulnerability, leaving you with the devastating weight of a sexual encounter without your consent. These experiences, these moments where our actions feel so far removed from our true selves, can leave us reeling in guilt, shame, and with a profound sense of self-betrayal.

"There is no light without shadow, and no psychic wholeness without imperfection. To round itself out, life calls not for perfection but for completeness; and for this, the inclusion of the 'shadow' is absolutely necessary."

– Carl Jung

The consequences of these actions, however they manifest, are an undeniable assault on your energy levels and your vibration. They create a disharmony within, a sense of being out of alignment with your core identity. These are the experiences that form those dark places inside, the shadows we try so desperately to deny. We tell ourselves, "That wasn't really me," because deep down, we know we are a good person. We believe that the trauma made us do it, and in a way, it did. But this is where the path can become slippery, leading us towards a place where we inadvertently become a victim of our own story.

If any of this content is triggering, remember your grounding tools such as Dropping Anchor and 4-7-8 Breathing. They will help you come back to your centre.

🔍 Falling into Victimhood

Playing the victim role, while understandable as a response to what feels like bottomless hurt, is a place where our energy stagnates and our light dims. It's a space where we inadvertently give our power away, relinquishing our agency to the past and its lingering effects. It breeds a sense of hopelessness, reinforcing the feeling of being stuck, forever defined by what happened *to* us, rather than who we are capable of becoming, our Future Self.

This victimhood can sadly reinforce those old, damaging messages from childhood – the ones that whispered you weren't enough, weren't good enough, weren't worthy. These whispers manifest as a relentless inner critic, fuelling negative self-talk and a toxic brew of negative emotions like resentment and bitterness. And in this stagnant pool of energy, there is no room for personal growth, no space for proper healing, no path forward towards the liberated woman you yearn to be. But accountability and responsibility for your unfiltered, whole self, shadows and all, is what is going to set you free.

Tragically, this place of victimhood is another driver that often fuels our need for quick fixes, or automatic behaviours with food and drink. The very parts of ourselves we are desperately trying to hide from – those shadow moments, those actions we regret – become the same things we try to numb with overeating, with processed foods that offer fleeting comfort, with alcohol that promises escape but delivers only deeper shadows. The desire to disappear, to hide away from our own perceived flaws, can create a cycle of extreme behaviours, followed by even more denial, and perhaps a tangled web of lies and deceit to mask what is actually happening within.

Needless to say, my friend, living in this cycle is miles away from living in alignment with your values and embodying the woman who is wholly

> "The avoidance of suffering is a form of suffering. The denial of pain is a form of pain."
> — Gabor Maté

liberated from her past. The woman who owns her energy, sets beautiful boundaries, and walks with her head held high, not in denial of her past but in courageous acceptance of her whole self – shadows and all. Now, *that's* taking responsibility, isn't it!

Building New Friendship Skills

Making friends with our shadows is such a tender and essential journey. It's so *not* about banishing them but about understanding they're a part of our whole, beautiful story.

Here are five easy steps to help you begin this heartfelt process

1. Create a Safe Space for Gentle Observation
Remember the quiet, cosy corner of your heart you created before? Here is where you can invite those shadowy parts to be seen. No judgement, no fixing, just a soft, loving curiosity. Maybe it's during your morning routine, that precious quiet time, or in the stillness before sleep, when the world is silent. Just a few moments to gently notice what feelings or thoughts tend to linger in the corners – the shame, the anger, the fear. It's like turning on a soft, dim light in a room you've kept dark for too long, just to see what's there without startling it, without making it run away.

2. Listen with Kindness and Curiosity
Instead of pushing those shadowy feelings away (which is your usual go-to, isn't it?), try leaning in with a sense of open curiosity.

Ask yourself, "What is this feeling really trying to tell me?" or "When have I felt this way before, in my life?" That embarrassing thing you did as a response to a trigger.

You only did what you did because of the tools and resources you had available at that moment, and that's absolutely okay, my friend; believe that. Often, these shadows are carrying unhealed wounds or unmet needs from our past. Treat them like a dear, dear friend who's hurting and wants to be heard, truly heard. You don't have to agree with everything they say, of course, but acknowledging their presence with genuine kindness can begin to dissolve their power over you, bit by bit.

3. Acknowledge the "Why" Behind the Shadow

Remember, these shadowy parts of yourself often developed as coping mechanisms, ways you tried to survive those difficult experiences that life throws at you. That anger might have been a fierce protector when you felt utterly powerless. That tendency to withdraw might have been a way to feel safe when the world felt overwhelmingly too much. Understanding the "why" behind these shadows, with compassion and with your whole heart, can help you move from harsh judgement to gentle acceptance. They were trying to help you, in their own way – the only way they knew how.

4. Find the Gold Within the Shadow

It might sound surprising, even a little strange, but even in our darkest, most secret corners, there can be hidden gems. That intense anger might also hold a fierce, burning passion for justice. That tendency to withdraw might also have a deep, thought-provoking capacity for introspection and self-awareness. What's the message in the mess? What is the learning opportunity here? What is this teaching you about yourself? By gently exploring your shadows, with an open heart and mind, you can often uncover unexpected lessons and strengths and integrate them into your whole, beautiful self. It's like finding a beautiful but tarnished piece of jewellery; with a bit of care, a little polish, its true brilliance can shine through, even brighter than before.

5. Practise Self-Compassion Every Step of the Way

This journey of befriending your shadows is a tender one, a delicate dance, and there will be times when it feels uncomfortable, even painful. Be incredibly gentle with yourself, my friend. Remind yourself again that healing takes time, that it's not a race, and that it's okay to stumble, to take a step back, to need a break. Just as you have offered your Former Self/Inner Child openness and kindness, acceptance and love, and an abundance of validation, offer this new friendship with your shadow self the same. In this new friendship, you will find a glimmer of light, a new energy conveying a different message – "You are worthy of this compassion. You are beautiful in every way." How wild would that be?!

Remember, my brave friend, making friends with your shadows is about becoming whole, genuinely whole. It's about embracing all of you, the light and the dark, with open arms and an open heart. And as you do, you'll find that your energy begins to flow more freely, your authenticity shines brighter than ever before, and a more profound sense of homegrown peace and joy blossoms within you. This joy comes from knowing and loving yourself completely.

> Being in love with yourself means accepting all parts of yourself, yes? Warts and all.

17.
Reflection Time

Unearthing Your Truths
Questions for Growth and Reclamation

My friend, you've taken some courageous steps to reach this point. I know this chapter – dealing with the parts of ourselves we hide – is hard, and it's certainly not pretty stuff. But please, stick with me. I want to guide you through this process in a transformative way, helping you finally make peace with your shadows.

As always, remember this is not about judgement; it's about connecting to the parts of yourself you've been taught to hide, okay? This path to your Liberated Connection requires you to bring all of yourself into the light.

Your role here is to allow these questions to illuminate the origins of behaviours that no longer serve you, helping you to clearly understand the link between old hurts and present-day choices. We are focused on observation, not reliving the pain. If you feel unsettled, know you have your 4-7-8 breathing and dropping anchor to ground you. Allow this process to open the door to deep awareness, whatever colour it may be, so true growth can occur.

Grab your favourite journal and let the words flow. As you explore these moments, remember that self-acceptance and self-compassion are your most important tools. I want you to get comfortable with the idea of befriending your shadows, as this is what empowers you to take actionable steps towards a deeper connection with your authenticity and your Future Self.

Remember to read all the questions and your written answers aloud – connecting with the sound of your own voice brings the truth into your body and mind.

Let's Begin

1. Can you gently recall a moment, maybe a whisper from your past, where you acted in a way that still brings a hint of shame or regret? What feeling comes up as you briefly bring that memory into the light?

2. Have you ever recognised, deep down, that a choice you made or a reaction you had was driven by a desire to avoid a painful emotion, only to end up facing a new layer of hurt or disappointment? Can you identify the emotion you were trying to outrun?

3. Reflecting on your shadows, are there specific parts of yourself, such as behaviours or reactions that stem from past trauma, that you often try to hide or deny, even from yourself? What stories do you tell to keep these parts hidden away?

4. Consider the idea of victimhood as we discussed. Can you identify any areas in your life where you might have unconsciously taken on this role, perhaps feeling powerless or defined only by what happened to you? What subtle signs might this be showing in your thoughts, language, or choices?

5. Reflect on how these shadow moments and any feelings of victimhood might affect your energy and emotional health. Do you notice a link between these hidden parts of yourself and feelings of stagnation, low vibration, or disconnection from your authentic self?

Here are five evoking questions about how you might take active steps to change behaviours:

1. If you were to extend a hand of compassion and understanding towards one of your shadow aspects, that part of yourself you've been hesitant to face, what small act of acceptance or acknowledgment could you offer it today?

2. Considering the cycle of attempting to avoid painful emotions through automatic behaviours, what is one small, conscious pause you could take the next time you feel that familiar urge arise, creating a space to choose a different response?

3. If you are prepared to gently move away from lingering feelings of victimhood, what is one small act of reclaiming your personal power – a tiny decision you make for yourself, a boundary you set, a voice you use – that would signal a shift towards being true to yourself?

4. Reflecting on the influences that lower your vibration (as discussed earlier), what is one small yet meaningful step you could take to consciously reduce some chaos in your life (perhaps by distancing yourself from a person or situation that consistently drains your energy), creating more space for calm and allowing your own luminous energy to flourish?

5. Thinking about practices that boost your vibration (like gratitude, nature, or creative expression), what is one small, purposeful action you could include in your daily routine this week that would truly nourish your energy and help you resonate at a higher frequency?

...

After the Reflection

When you read all those questions and your answers out loud, I am sure there will be something that has been sparked within you.

For sure, it sounds like this part of our journey together has gently nudged you to peek into those shadowed corners, those bits of yourself you often tuck away. It takes such courage to even glance in their direction, doesn't it? But perhaps you're finding, as you sit with these reflections, that these shadows aren't monsters in the dark, but rather pieces of your whole, intricate story. Maybe you're starting to see that these experiences, though painful, have shaped the incredible person you are today — resilient, wise, and so deeply human.

Now, as you carry this newfound understanding, remember this: You are inherently worthy of love, worthy to feel your beautiful energy flow through every single part of you, in your peaceful, joyous place in the world. There's no need to banish those shadows; instead, can you learn to hold them with compassion, like you would a dear friend who's been through a tough time?

> **"Owning our story and loving ourselves through that process is the bravest thing that we'll ever do."**
>
> – Brené Brown.

Keep moving forward, my friend, with an open heart and the knowledge that you are seen, you are valued, and you are becoming more beautifully you with every step.

You're not defined by the moments you regret, but by the strength and grace you bring to each new breath and step you take.

I'm still here, holding your hand.

A Note

A sidebar between us girls...

Don't be surprised if your perception of the world begins to soften, to expand. This is your capacity for new things coming in. It's like a weird awakening of sorts. It is slow, and then it's not – a wild new unveiling of a broader reality.

Embrace this mental expansion, my friend. If you can find your way back to your Inner Child to release those old narratives and wounded beliefs, life will shift. Changes will happen. Those old, ingrained notions of what's "normal" will become a thing of the past. Sure, there will be challenges along the way, and at times it will feel like all of this is too difficult. But, please, keep with it; that is when the breakthroughs happen. This is where you start to experience what it feels like in your own liberated connection.

Perhaps this is where you let go of those people who live "without connection" to their true selves. They supposedly can't perceive anything other than to fit in with the masses. Which is not who you are anymore.

In your newfound liberation, you're unlocking a whole new dimension of life. It's akin to stepping through an invisible veil into a very real, quite often breathtaking, home-grown garden of whatever colour of peace and joy you choose it to be.

> Here's the thing: Short-term fixes come with long-term costs. You'll see that accepting a small amount of discomfort now is manageable and guarantees significant long-term advantages. This can all be your new normal if you allow it to be.

The Art of Intentional Creation

18. Manifesting Your Deepest Desires

Guiding Your Energy for Joyful Purpose
From Reaction to Conscious Creation

Now, my dear friend, after all that incredible work you've done in untangling the past and understanding your energy connection, it's time to set your sights on the horizon – on creating the life your heart genuinely yearns for. And guess what? This isn't about some grand, overwhelming quest; it's about gently guiding your energy towards what you genuinely desire, allowing it to flow with joy and purpose.

Think of it this way: for too long, so much of your precious energy might have been caught up in those old cycles, those shadows of the past. Now, we're shifting gears. We're moving from simply reacting to life to actively *creating* the experiences you long for. It's like redirecting a powerful stream; instead of letting it get stuck in stagnant pools, we're guiding it towards lush, alluring landscapes. And, yes, my friend, even your relationship with food and drink gets to play a harmonious role in this beautiful unfolding.

This journey of getting what you want is deeply connected to those values you so thoughtfully identified. Remember them? They're like your inner compass, always pointing you towards what feels genuinely aligned. Now, we're extending that consciousness. We're asking: in different areas of your life – your relationships, your work (that thing that lights you up!), your mental and physical health – what is it that you *really* want? And how can you consciously direct your energy and actions to bring those desires to life, in a way that feels good and honours who you are?

> **"The future belongs to those who believe in the beauty of their dreams."**
>
> – Eleanor Roosevelt

For instance, are you dreaming of a loving, connected relationship? Wonderful! What small, brave steps can you take, fuelled by your desire, while also being mindful of how food and drink might play a part in those early dates or deeper connections? When you take the reins like this, your energy naturally aligns with that intention. It's like sending a clear signal out into the universe, saying, "This is what my heart desires, and I'm moving towards it with clarity and joy."

Now, to make this feel less like a chore and more like an exciting exploration, let's pick an area of your life where you'd love to see some positive movement. Maybe it's your health – wanting to feel more vibrant and energised. Or perhaps it's your work – longing for a sense of purpose and fulfilment. It could even be nurturing deeper intimacy. Whatever it is, let's focus there for a moment. What are those little milestones, those joyful achievements you'd love to experience in that area?

Think about it – if it's intimacy, what are the values you want to shine through in your connections? Honesty? Vulnerability? Playfulness? Choosing values that resonate deeply with you will not only help you get what you want but will also ensure you're building intimacy on a foundation of self-worth and integrity. There are countless ways to reach your desires, my friend, but the most empowering path is the one that lifts you higher, not the one that makes you question your beautiful self.

And now, for a little bit of playful structure to help your wonderful energy move in the right direction, let me introduce you to a tool called S.M.A.R.T. Now, hold on a second! This isn't some stiff, corporate goal-setting thing. We're giving it our own lovely twist, making it a fun and effective way to map out your desires.

Your S.M.A.R.T. Path to Joyful Manifestation

Welcome to the new and energetically improved S.M.A.R.T. guide – your easy guide and playful checklist to help you take those brave steps towards what your heart truly wants, all while keeping your energy flowing beautifully. Think of it as adding a little sparkle and intention to your heart's desire!

S.M.A.R.T. is all about making those desires feel tangible and achievable, helping you live in alignment with your values, and gently nudging you away from those old habits that might dim your shine. It might feel a little like a fun experiment at first, but soon enough, it'll become your natural way of weaving my way towards joy.

So, what does our wonderfully reimagined S.M.A.R.T. guide look like?

S – Be Specific
(Get Crystal Clear on Your Heart's Whisper!)

Instead of a vague wish like "I want to be loved," let's get laser-focused on what that *truly* means for your energy. What does that connection look and feel like in your heart and body? Imagine the experience fully. What's happening? Who are you with (it could be yourself!)? What kind of energy are you sharing and receiving? Write down all the vivid details of this desired connection. For instance, try: "I will consciously set aside fifteen minutes each day to genuinely listen to my inner voice without distraction, noticing the soft nudges of my intuition. And when I'm with loved ones, I will put away my phone and offer them my full, present attention, feeling the warmth of our shared energy." See how much clearer that intention feels? It's like tuning into a precise frequency, allowing your energy to align with exactly what you're seeking. Be specific – that way, you direct your energy with intention.

M – Motivated by Your Values
(Let Your Inner Compass Lead!)

This is where your beautiful inner compass comes in! Make sure your desires are deeply connected to what really matters to you. Wanting a loving relationship because you value connection and intimacy? Yes! Wanting something because you think you *should* want it? Or wanting a relationship because you are scared to be alone, or you feel like less of a person because everyone else has a partner? Perhaps you can gently explore that. When your desires align with your values, your energy feels naturally aligned and powerful.

This is where your beautiful, unique values shine, my friend! Does this desire allow you to be authentic? Will you trust yourself and feel confident with your boundaries? Does it feel aligned with the woman you're becoming, that radiant Future Self you're stepping into? Every time you're setting your sights on something, check in with your inner compass. Does it point towards those core values you've chosen? When your actions are fuelled by what really matters to you, your energy flows with passion and purpose. And, then authentically, it feels right, doesn't it?

A – Be Adaptive
(Flow Like Water, My Dear!)

Life has its own rhythm, and sometimes our plans need a little wiggle room. Is this desire something that feels like it will genuinely enhance your life, something you can weave into your days in a way that feels natural and good? Can you be flexible and adjust your approach if things shift? Think of it as dancing with life – sometimes you lead, sometimes you follow, but you're always moving forward. If something feels like a constant uphill battle draining your energy, maybe it's time to gently adapt your approach.

R – Be Realistic
(And Oh-So Kind to Yourself!)

Dream as big as your heart desires, my friend! But let's also be real and practical with the steps you take. What do you need to make this happen? Do you have the time, the energy, the support, the know-how? It's okay if you don't have everything right now. Maybe one of your first steps is to *get* what you need, whether it's learning a new skill or asking for support. Be honest with yourself, without judgement. If a big dream feels overwhelming, break it down into smaller, kinder steps that feel energising and achievable. Celebrate those little victories – they keep your inner fire burning!

T – Time-Conscious
(Give Your Dreams a Date to Bloom!)

When do you want to see this beautiful thing come to life? Give it a timeframe, my friend. It doesn't have to be rigid, but having a sense of when you'd like to move forward helps you commit your energy and focus. Be realistic with your timelines – we humans have a funny way of underestimating how long things take, and then we can be so hard on ourselves for not meeting those self-imposed deadlines. Be gentle but set an intention. It's like planting a seed – you have an idea of when you hope to see it sprout.

Remember, embracing a little playful structure with S.M.A.R.T. isn't about becoming rigid or losing your wonderful spontaneity. It's about giving your incredible energy a clear direction, a loving framework to move within as you consciously create the life your heart truly desires. It's about gently taking the reins and guiding your precious energy towards the joy, peace, and fulfilment you so deeply deserve.

> "A woman with a voice is by definition a strong woman."
> – Melinda Gates

You've refined the new script, you've connected with your inner voice, and you've ignited your vibrant energy. The stage is set, my friend. You are the strong, radiant lead in your own magnificent story, and you absolutely deserve to get everything your heart desires. Now, off you go, and shine!

Never underestimate the powerful energy of a woman who knows what she wants!

Nurturing Your Inner Garden
The Art of Energetic Practice

Sweet friend, remember that beautiful vision you have for your life, that radiant Future Self you're stepping into? Getting there, living by your deepest values, allowing life's little storms to pass without reaching for old numbing habits – it all blossoms through practice.

Think of practice not as a chore but as tending to your inner garden. Just like a seed needs consistent watering and sunlight to grow strong, your energetic skills need regular attention to start to flourish.

So, what does "energetic practice" look like for you? Remember that wonderful work you did, understanding your values to improve your relationships and gently shift those unwanted patterns? Once you've nurtured that area and feel a beautiful sense of your own power there, what's the next patch of your inner garden you'd like to nurture?

Perhaps it's your connection to your intuition, that quiet inner knowing. Maybe it's strengthening your ability to set loving boundaries or deepening your grounding practices. It could even be consciously cultivating more joy and laughter in your daily life. The possibilities are endless, my friend!

When you consciously define how you want to nurture these aspects of yourself and how you're going to cultivate them actively, *you* become the loving gardener of your own energy. *You* are steering your ship, pointing yourself towards the vibrant life you deserve.

And when you're in the driver's seat like that, the role of anything that might temporarily distract or numb you – food, drink, old coping mechanisms – naturally shifts. They no longer hold the steering wheel because *you* do. And when those inevitable emotional storms roll in, you'll be more anchored, more able to gently weather them because you know your destination, you know the vibrant energy you're cultivating within.

> "It's not getting what you want that's the hard part; it's deciding what you want."
> – Alexandra Potter

It's a simple truth, my friend – humans feel lost without a map. Imagine wandering in a dense forest without any direction – you'd likely walk in circles, wouldn't you? It's the same with your precious energy. You become especially vulnerable when those old triggers arise if you haven't consciously set your course, if you haven't practised connecting to your inner guidance and your grounding anchors. That's when you risk falling back into those familiar loops, and that's when those old numbing habits might try to take control again.

So, how does that feel? Do you think you could feel a little spark of motivation now? Imagine the incredible sense of inner strength, feeling as though you are standing on solid ground for once. Gosh, imagine what could blossom in your life as you consistently practise these empowering, energetic skills. The possibilities are endless.

∞ Allow Your Future Self to Be Your Energetic Compass

Still feeling a little foggy on what you want to work on? No worries at all, my friend! Sometimes the path isn't crystal clear right away. If you're feeling a little unsure where to focus your energetic practice, let's revisit that beautiful vision of your Future Self. Remember all those wonderful qualities and experiences you envisioned for her?

Take a loving look at how you imagine her living, how she feels: What practices might support that? Maybe she feels deeply connected to her intuition – that might inspire you to practise quiet meditation or journalling.

Perhaps she had strong, loving boundaries – that could lead you to practise saying "no" with kindness and clarity.

Let's gently break those down, one by one, and see what skills you might want to practise to bring those elements into your present reality. Don't overthink it, my friend!

> **NOTE:** Use the S.M.A.R.T. framework we explored earlier to bring a newfound structure to your energetic practice.
>
> Be **Specific** about the skill you want to strengthen. Let it be **Motivated** by your Values, those beautiful treasures you've claimed as your own. Be **Adaptive**, allowing your practice to evolve as you do. Be **Realistic** and kind to yourself about the time and energy you have. And be **Time-Conscious**, setting very specific intentions for when and how often you'll engage in your practice.
>
> **Remember, my friend, when you dedicate time to your energetic practice, you are prioritising *yourself*.** You are choosing your own emotional, physical, and energetic balance over people-pleasing or old obligations that drain your energy. You are building those vital inner muscles that help you stay grounded and true to yourself, no matter what life throws your way.

This is incredibly important work. It's about building a resilient foundation of self-awareness and energetic mastery. So, let's embrace the beautiful journey, my friend. With each conscious breath, each moment of grounding, each loving boundary you set, you are cultivating a more vibrant, peaceful, and liberated you. Keep tending that inner garden – you are worth every bit of loving care.

Practice doesn't make you perfect; we know that no one is perfect, right? Practice is progress. Practice is improvement.

> Practice is becoming free and being the woman you want to be, metaphorically skipping through the daisies, lapping up your home-grown peace and joy.

Clearing the Path
The Energetic Solution to Values Conflict

We've already explored the animated power that flows within you when your energy is clear, haven't we? But life, as we both know, rarely unfolds in a perfectly straight, linear fashion.

What happens when that beautiful flow hits a snag, when it encounters resistance, and the path forward feels completely blocked? More often than not, the culprit is a conflict with your values. When your actions, or the circumstances you find yourself in, clash with what you sincerely believe in, it creates awful friction. This internal struggle dims your light, drains your focus, and hinders the natural, beautiful expression of your authentic self.

But here is the empowering truth: you possess an innate, incredible ability to navigate these turbulent waters. The secret to resolution lies in knowing which energy to call upon at each stage of the process.

> **"Be deliberate in your decision and execution. Your integrity depends on your willingness to align what you know with what you do."**
>
> — Dr. Henry Cloud

A Dance of Resolution: Masculine Meets Feminine

Resolving a values conflict is not a rigid, multi-step chore; it's a fluid, powerful dance between your two core energies.

🔗 1. The Feminine Path: Acceptance, Insight, and Healing

The journey begins with your Feminine Energy, providing the essential vulnerability and acceptance. It offers the capacity to feel and understand the conflict, stopping the immediate energetic drain.

The Feminine Energy teaches you to:

- **Accept the Reality:** Gently acknowledge the conflict's presence without resistance or judgement. Fighting against what is only dissipates your precious energy.

- **Normalise and Process:** Embrace your emotions, reminding yourself that anxiety or overwhelm are temporary messengers. Use breathwork and connect to your **Values Choice Point** (the moment before you react or make a choice to live by your values) to anchor yourself in the present moment, creating space for the emotions without letting them become the decision-maker.

- **Reflect with Compassion:** Engage in honest self-inquiry on your own role in the situation, illuminating the conflict's underlying truth. The Feminine Energy encourages you to release the illusion of a perfect resolution, treating any misstep as valuable feedback, not a failure.

- **Heal and Nurture:** Envelop yourself in deep compassion, making choices that nurture your body, mind, and spirit. This is the healing phase, illuminating the truth and restoring energetic clarity.

2. The Masculine Path: Discipline, Choice, and Action

Once the truth is illuminated, your Masculine Energy provides the structure and discipline required to implement lasting change. It gives you the unwavering focus to act and commit.

The Masculine Energy teaches you to:

- **Mindfully Weigh Costs:** Take a thoughtful pause to consider the realistic costs of inaction versus the potential benefits of aligning with your values. The Masculine Energy asks: What path will ultimately bring me closer to my core self?

- **Commit to Value-Driven Action:** Make a conscious commitment to act in a way that honours your core values. Remember that inaction is also a choice, and often carries a far greater cost in the long run.

- **Stand Firm:** Once a choice is made, stand firm in its intention. Be loyal to your process, especially when external noise resists your boundary. If the outcome is imperfect, view it as feedback to recalibrate, not a reason for retreat.

By consciously engaging with value conflicts through this thoughtful dance – using the Feminine to understand and the Masculine to implement – you are actively clearing the path for your pure, radiant energy to flow unimpeded.

Living in alignment with your values is the very essence of harnessing your radiant energy, guiding you towards a life filled with greater peace, joy, and sincere authenticity.

Make choices that simply nurture your body, mind, and spirit, aligning with your values, rather than seeking temporary escapes that further disconnect you from your authentic energy. (Alcohol has such a dampening effect on your energy and is a sure-fire way to lower your vibration, making you vulnerable to energy vampires.)

> **"Every conflict we face in life is rich with positive and negative potential ... The choice is not up to our opponents, but to us, and our willingness to face and work through them."**
> – Kenneth Cloke

Engage in the best loving-myself-actions that work for you; this way, you will learn how to quickly uplift your vibration and get back to the home-grown happiness and joy.

Remember, your Former Self (Inner Child) and Future Self are your biggest inner cheerleaders, ready to see this evocative flow emerge triumphantly.

19.
Reflection Time

Charting Your Course for Forward Motion
Questions for Clarity and Confident Action

My friend, we are now going to channel that deep awareness into forward motion – into creating the reality of who you want to be, the authentic Future Self who has been waiting for you.

The liberation you're building is not just about healing old wounds; it's about making space for what you truly desire, in a real, raw, and honest way. This section is your chance to move beyond the boundaries of past behaviours and fears, and to consciously align your energy with your unrealised goals and ambitions.

Your role here is to allow these questions to illuminate the possibility within you. We'll gently dissect the internal barriers that once held you back, replacing those old 'Why Not?' narratives with the truth coming forth by your 'Yes, You Can!' anthem. You are focused on intentional creation, not reliving old doubts.

Grab your favourite journal and see how your inner voice spills out onto the page. As you explore these moments, be your own guide, your own coach, and your own validation. You know that compassion and softness are your friends. This intentional exploration is what empowers you to take concrete, actionable steps towards a deeper connection with your authenticity, moving you closer to the woman you are meant to be.

Let this exercise be a compass, guiding your precious energy towards your desires, towards change, and towards getting what you want in life. Knowing you made all this happen, homegrown and aligned with feeling good in your skin.

I am sure I don't need to remind you that reading all questions and your answers aloud brings connection within and sparks the desire for change.

Off you go …

Let's Begin

1. **Whispers of Your Heart:** Think about that one dream, that desire you've maybe tucked away, the "thing/goal/ambition" your Future Self keeps reminding you about. What has held you back from stepping towards it? And what's the very first, tiny spark of energy that ignites within you when you even *imagine* moving towards it?

2. **The "Why Not?" Chorus:** Oh, that busy mind of yours! What are some of the familiar tunes it plays – the "reasons why you can't", the things you shouldn't do. Or even the "I can't do that" narrative that has kept you stuck in the past when you've considered going after what you truly want? Write them down with kindness, acknowledging their presence without giving them too much power.

3. **The "Yes, You Can!" Anthem:** Now, listen closely to the steady voice of your magnificent Future Self. What encouraging words, what powerful truths does she whisper about your ability to achieve this goal or aspiration? What does she see in you that perhaps you're only just beginning to fully grasp?

4. **Unpacking the Past's Baggage:** Consider those challenging thoughts and feelings that have acted as barriers in the past – the anxiety that constricts your chest, the anger that ignites, the insecurity that whispers doubts. Can you gently "name and tame" one or two of these, recognising their presence without allowing them to shape your path forward? What's one small way you can show yourself a bit more kindness and understanding when they arise again?

5. **Your S.M.A.R.T. Compass:** Take that thing/goal/ambition you're holding in your heart: How can you use our wonderfully reimagined S.M.A.R.T. compass to map out a very specific first step? What's one **Specific** action you can take, fuelled by what's truly

Meaningful to you? How can you stay **Adaptive** along the way, be **Realistic** with your energy, and give it a loving **Timeframe** in which to begin to bloom? Then, notice and observe how even that small step can shift your energy from feeling stuck to gently flowing forward.

6. **The Guiding Light of Your Values:** Which of your chosen values feels most connected to this goal or ambition? How can you consciously incorporate behaviours that honour these values into your journey, knowing they will help you achieve your desire and keep your energy aligned and genuine? Trust and authenticity will provide the inner clarity needed to protect your energy in every situation.

7. **The Ripple Effect of "Yes!":** Imagine, for a moment, having already achieved this thing/goal/ambition. What are the *real* benefits that ripple through your life? How will it feel in your body, in your heart, in your daily experiences? Remember, even the smallest positive shifts can create a beautiful wave of energy.

8. **Navigating the Bumps in the Road:** As we've discussed before, life has its small detours, doesn't it? What are some potential conflicts or challenges that might arise as you work towards your desired outcome? Consider unsupportive voices, time pressures, or old habits that might try to resurface. How can you use your new skills to prepare for these, perhaps by applying the boundary-setting techniques you've been practising? Connecting with those genuine benefits can be a strong source of motivation and a lovely way to lift your vibration.

9. **Your Future Self's Cheerleading Squad:** Imagine your wise and loving Future Self standing beside you right now. What encouraging words, what unwavering support does she offer as you embark on this journey? What simple steps does she remind you to take to prioritise your own beautiful energy along the way?

Let those words sink into your heart and become a source of energising support.

10. **Your Heart's Promise:** Taking all of this into consideration, can you commit to yourself that you will take one small, brave action towards your thing/goal/ambition? Perhaps even knowing that mistakes are just part of the beautiful unfolding of your journey? What do you feel is in your reach that you could do to honour your desire and direct your precious energy towards this intention? What feels like *your* truth right now? Whisper that commitment to yourself, my friend.

•••

After Your Reflection

My dearest friend, as you take these reflections on board, remember this: Every tiny step you take forward, no matter how small it may seem, is a victory. Please, show yourself some praise and appreciation for each one.

Whisper, "Well done, (use your name)," pat yourself on the back with genuine warmth, and let yourself feel impressed by your own courage and commitment. This gentle encouragement is the enforcing energy that will keep your vibration high, nourish your inner garden, and inspire you to keep reaching for what your truest self desires.

This feeling of progress is a definite tonic, no doubt. Sometimes, it'll take a while to truly sink in. These questions may not give you any instant gratification, so just remember that. Your brain needs time to reorganise things, and you need time to accept this notion of energetic liberation truly. Your once very active, hyper-attuned approach to life has been in charge for a very long time. Change takes some time and patience.

> **"The privilege of a lifetime is to become who you truly are."**
> – Carl Jung

BUT!!! You're making space for change. I know I keep saying this, very deliberately, I might add. As you see your own growth, more shifts occur. This is where subtle changes happen in your ability to see yourself differently. A deeper, raw, and genuine belief in yourself and your new skills and abilities will start to show itself through your new automatic ways. Making this "trusting oneself" business even easier!

Just like watering a garden, tracking your progress helps you see how far you've come and what beauty will start to bloom before you. So, in whatever way feels good to you – a few notes in a journal, a quiet acknowledgment at the end of the day – keep a learned eye on your Change Experience journey.

And, yes, my friend, I can say from experience that this beautiful unfolding really does take practice, like all new skills do. Be patient and kind with yourself. Don't be afraid of the wobbles or the stumbles; they are simply part of the dance. As you become more familiar with these tools, you will begin to simply savour the empowering feeling of your own progress.

Can't wait for you to tap into all these newfound energetic and very magical superpowers. Keep shining, my friend; I see you.

Your Liberation Toolbox 2.0

20.
The Superpowers Continue

Six Skills for an Effortless Life
Calling in the Magic

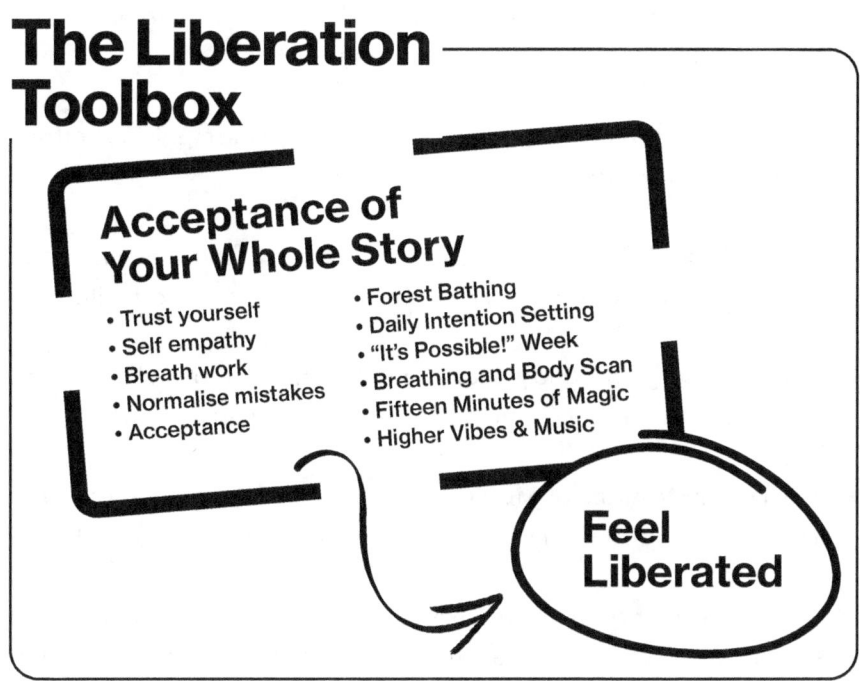

Alright, my friend, take a moment and genuinely reflect on how far you've come! Remember the foundations we built together in Book Two: *A New Perspective*'s toolbox? You gathered the essentials, but now, standing here on this beautiful threshold, it's time for an energetic upgrade.

> **"Life isn't about finding yourself. Life is about creating yourself."**
> — George Bernard Shaw

You've done the deep, soulful work to clear the path. Now, we're calling in the magic and the must-have life skills to ensure your most liberated life feels effortless, protected, and fun! This isn't just about coping; this is about equipping you with six brand-new superpowers to actively shape your destiny and keep your vibration soaring.

These are the essential practices I rely on every single day to keep my cup full, my energy field strong, and my intentions unfolding with grace.

Get ready to add the six new superpowers to your Liberation Toolbox 2.0:

1. Forest Bathing: Tapping into Mother Earth's high, pure energy for profound healing and energetic rebalancing.

2. Daily Intention Setting: Consciously calling in the magic and effortlessly directing your day towards your desires.

3. "It's Possible!" Week: A playful dare to unleash your inhibitions and swap "no" for "It could be possible ..." to open up to new opportunities.

4. Breathing and Body Scan: Your instant dose of calm and the quickest way to find your centre and soothe your nervous system.

5. Fifteen Minutes of Magic: Using movement and a mini scan to maintain energetic equilibrium and elevate your vibration every single day.

6. Higher Vibrations Through Music: Connecting your energy field to sound to release stagnant energy and invite feelings of pure joy and freedom.

You'll see in the coming pages I call four, five, and six the "Three Pillars of Presence," because that's exactly what they are – they're all about helping you be more present. This is about you, in your full energetic power, stepping forward and claiming the glorious, easy life you deserve.

Let's dive in and master these tools together!

🔗 One: Opening Your Energetic Senses
Forest Bathing Uplifting Connection in Nature

Alright, my friend, let's gently shake off any lingering heaviness and lift our gaze towards the bigger picture – the concept of energy at large.

You know by now that our personal landscapes are painted by the unique brushstrokes of our experiences, right? Our upbringing, the wonderful and weird people we've encountered, and the moments that have etched themselves onto our hearts all intertwine to create the unique tapestry of who we are. And here's a truth that resonates deep within – we are all interconnected threads in a vast, pulsing, energetic web.

Your Body is Wise: Sensing the Current

Energy, my friend, is not some ethereal whisper; it's real, it's solid, tangible, and it's a fundamental force. When you walk into a room, you instantly sense the vibe – the lightness and joy of someone vibrant, or the subtle pressure and unease that clings to a person carrying heavy energy. That's you, feeling the tangible presence of another's energetic field. And, yes, while high energy can feel exhilarating, remember that intensity isn't always positive; sometimes, it can be the sharp edge of negativity.

> **"If you wish to know the divine, feel the wind on your face and the warm sun on your hand."**
> – Buddha

That knot in your stomach, that sudden headache in someone's presence – your body is wise; it's picking up on those stronger, sometimes contradictory, vibrations. Just as you can discern the "bad vibes," you can feel the uplifting "good vibes" from a kind soul who makes you smile inside.

The energy of nature operates on this similar principle, but it is amplified and purified. It vibrates at a much higher, cleaner, and more balanced frequency. Nature's energy is like a luscious body cream, penetrating deep into your soul – it is a powerful, harmonious force, abundant and free, simply waiting for you to open your heart and mind to receive it. It requires only a gentle shift in perspective, a willingness to be quietly in tune with how your body feels when immersed in it.

🔍 Forest Bathing: Your Pathway to Deep Healing

Alright, this is the exciting part! I'm keen to share one of my absolute favourite ways to boost my health and happiness. I credit a lot of my vibrant, high-energy vibe to a beautiful, mindful practice called Forest Bathing, or as the Japanese refer to it, Shinrin-Yoku. Shinrin means "forest," and Yoku means "bath," so it literally means "bathing in the forest atmosphere."

This isn't just a brisk walk or a hike; it's a beautiful, intentional journey to reconnect with yourself and the incredible energy of nature. It's a mindful, sensory immersion – a way of truly being one with nature and allowing the forest to embrace you.

Imagine immersing yourself in the forest's atmosphere, engaging all your senses – sight, hearing, smell, touch, and even the subtle taste of the air. It's about slowing down and allowing yourself to truly feel everything around you. This conscious practice of opening your senses bridges the gap between you and the natural world, fostering a radical sense of connection with Mother Earth.

🔍 Why Japan Leads the Way to Healing

The Japanese recognised the profound health benefits of this practice decades ago, formalising it as a cornerstone of preventive public health. Why?

The incredible secret lies in the compounds the trees release, called phytoncides. These are nature's essential oils, and when inhaled, they actively and gently calm your nervous system.

> **"The forest is the therapist, and the trees are the healers."**
>
> – Amos Clifford

This is where the deep energetic work begins. By slowing down and opening your senses, you allow the forest's high, clean frequency to interact with your own. This natural, profound connection creates an environment where the lower, heavier frequencies of old inner wounds, trauma, and chronic mental clutter can finally begin to lift and disperse.

Beyond this deep emotional release, Shinrin-Yoku offers tangible physical benefits that bolster your energetic field. Studies have shown that time spent mindfully in the woods significantly boosts the activity of your Natural Killer (NK) cells, which are vital components of your immune system.

Your Immune System's Rapid Response Team

Now, you might be wondering, what exactly are these incredible Natural Killer (NK) cells that I'm talking about? Don't worry, we're not diving deep into a biology textbook, but this bit is so empowering, you need to know about it!

> **"Life is not happening to you. Life is responding to you."**
> — Rhonda Byrne

Think of your NK cells as the rapid response team of your personal energetic army. They are a special type of white blood cell whose sole mission is to constantly patrol your body, looking out for trouble. Unlike some other immune cells that need time to 'learn' about a threat, your NK cells are ready to act immediately. They specialise in quickly identifying and destroying any cells that have been infected by a virus (like that nasty cold) or cells that have turned cancerous. They are crucial for your body's frontline defence, and when they get a boost – like they do from a session of Forest Bathing – your whole defence system is dramatically strengthened.

Furthermore, it is proven to improve sleep quality and increase cognitive focus and creative ability, ensuring that when you step back into your life, you are more centred and capable. The forest holds a space of unwavering peace, allowing your heart and body to enter a healing resonance that is often difficult to find in your busy, everyday life.

A Global Invitation to Raise Your Vibration

What started as a national movement in Japan has now become a worldwide phenomenon. Recognised by practitioners and health services across the globe, Forest Bathing is used as a powerful, non-pharmacological way to reduce stress hormones, lower blood pressure, and truly uplift the soul.

It's about letting go of that mental clutter – stresses, worries, and the absorbing of other people's draining energy – and being fully present in the moment. With this simple lens shift, you exchange the chaos of daily life for profound inner peace, allowing nature's universal energy to flow freely into your own energetic field.

> Happy connecting to, and raising your vibrations, my friend!

 **AN INTERESTING NOTE:** Human DNA emits light. When vibrational frequencies are high – such as when someone is experiencing love, the calming effect of nature, or the presence of someone with a strong, loving frequency – that light grows stronger.

Your Forest Bathing Instructions: A Simple Guide

- **Find Your Spot:** Seek out a place where you can walk aimlessly and slowly. It could be a forest, a park, or even a quiet garden.

- **Disconnect:** Put your phone in aeroplane mode (or better yet, leave it behind!) so you're not distracted by vibrations or notifications. This is your time to be fully present.

- **Glide and Sense:** Allow yourself to glide; let your senses guide you forward.

- **Follow Your Intuition:** Follow your intuition, breathe deeply, and give yourself the gift of time. There's no rush here.
- **It's Not About the Destination:** Where you go doesn't matter. This isn't about following a map or covering a certain amount of ground. It's about the experience.
- **Fill Your Cup:** Your purpose is to feel connected and fill your cup with all the beautiful sounds, smells, and sensations around you.
- **Listen to the Birds:** Take joy in listening to the birds singing their melodies.
- **Feel the Breeze:** Slow down and feel the breeze rustling in the leaves of the trees.
- **Smell the Forest:** Breathe in the fragrance of the forest – the grass, the moss, the delicate scents of the foliage.
- **Appreciate the Light:** Appreciate the beauty of the light filtering through the trees.
- **Savour the Freshness:** Savour the freshness of the air as you slow your breathing.
- **Connect Physically:** Hug a tree. Touch the foliage.
- **Flow with Water:** If there's a stream, birdbath, or puddle, put your hands in the water.
- **Soak It All In:** Soak up all the flavours of your surroundings.
- **Connect to the Energy:** As you immerse yourself in all this natural beauty, feel your energy connect with the energy of the forest.

... and don't forget to breathe!

The Next Part – International Energy
Liberated from Old Patterns, Empowered by a Higher Vibration

While you are connecting to the earth's energy, you may be asking, what does all of this have to do with helping you be the liberated woman you want to be? Can it help you stop those unwanted behaviours? The not-so-helpful ways you have used to distract yourself from your emotional pain? To help you evoke a desire to change the choices you make with food or drink to numb what feels off? Good question. It's about intention.

When you set an intention for the day, when you set your path and call in what you truly desire, you reduce the risk of falling off the wagon, of going off course, or of being thrown around by external circumstances. You've asked for what you want, and that clarity is a powerful anchor. This, my friend, is another superpower – one you will come to hold dear as you recognise its role in connecting you to balance in your life.

The second piece of this puzzle is understanding that when you're making changes, when you're deciding on the changes you want to embrace, you want your energy and vibration to be as high as possible. When your energy (your vibrational frequency) is low, you're more vulnerable to the strong negative energy of others. You might find yourself easily swayed by conflict or indecision.

> **"Those who contemplate the beauty of the earth find reserves of strength that will endure as long as life lasts."**
> – Rachel Carson

For me, as you have already gathered, a forest walk is my daily bread and butter. It gives me the light I need to boost my energy, that vitality that transforms my readiness for the day.

∞ Your Energetic Invitation: Just Try It

Let's focus on you now, my friend. I encourage you to intentionally explore the energy all around your home environment. (I appreciate you may not have a forest nearby.) Listen to the birdsong in the morning. Feel the solid earth beneath your feet. Listen to the sounds of trees reaching towards the skies. Feel the pull of the ocean, the soothing murmur of a flowing stream, or the crackle of a fire. Even a quiet moment spent in your local park can be a profound experience.

This is where the magic of grounding comes in. By consciously connecting with the earth – feeling the grass, the coolness of a stone – you instantly anchor your own energy. It's like tuning a radio to a clear, high-frequency station; you become less susceptible to lower vibrations and more receptive to nature's pure resonance. This simple act initiates a powerful, natural rebalancing within you.

So, take a deep, nourishing breath of that fresh air. Listen to the whispering leaves, the joyful chorus of birdsong. If water is near, let its gentle rhythm wash over you. Close your eyes and surrender to this "nature bath," a soothing elixir for the exhaustion from your core wounds.

Notice how you feel. Is a sense of calm settling in? A quiet smile blooming within. An appreciation for the beauty surrounding you. That's you, my friend, harmonising with the energy of the natural world and creating a stable foundation to maintain your higher vibration.

> Do you think you could give it a try and see if it works for you? Just try, okay, and remember to ask very specifically for what you want. It might feel uncomfortable at first, and you might need to practise it, but I can tell you, it's a basic practice that has become essential for me. Don't be intimidated to do this because of what someone else might think.

"The Earth has music for those who listen."
– William Shakespeare

When life feels overwhelming, allow yourself the grace to simply be with it. This journey is about slowing down just enough to truly feel life, to listen to the intuition within your body, and to connect with the boundless energy within and around you.

When you want to stand strong against the things that push you around, having this superpower of high energy means you can feel safe and confident. Your cup will be full, filled with the right energy. You can make a difference; you can make the change you desire. You have everything you need within you.

> It's time to reach in and claim it, my friend.

My Little Note

A little sidebar chat between us girls

If there's a place near you where you can go to ground yourself, where you can connect with nature, where you can be among trees – even hug a tree – find that place. Spend time there. Go for a walk. If possible, make it a part of your daily routine. If daily isn't feasible, aim for weekly. Giving yourself that earthy energy can only do you good. I'm a big believer in hugging trees. If you don't want to touch the tree, that is okay. I recommend giving it a "Reiki hug". Get close, reach your arms our like you want to give it a hug, and let yourself feel the energy exchange.

You just have to lean into this, and if you're sceptical, that's okay. The only way to really appreciate this is to experience it yourself. If it doesn't seem to work the first time, try again. The key is visualising the energy going into the pain point. Give it a colour if that helps. See the energy flowing. Focus.

> Uplift yourself with the pure energy from these magnificent trees, beings that have been here much longer than we have. What do you say? Could you give it a go?

My Forrest Cleansing Experience

I call this forest cleansing because my energy feels genuinely cleansed and refreshed after each morning walk. There's a powerful recharging that happens – the awakening of my senses: the smells, the sounds, the feeling of the air on my skin, and the sensations in my feet as I walk. It all has a magnetic pull. I'm sure you'll discover this beautiful, abundant flow when you try this practice.

To give you a little context, I walk in a forest every morning with my sweet dog, Peach (she's a gorgeous Groodle, by the way – a Golden Retriever mixed with a Poodle). It's a non-negotiable part of our day.

I always say "Hello" to the trees, the birds, and all the little critters we encounter. I start by sharing an affirmation with the universe, setting my intention about how the day will unfold and how "happy, healthy, and safe" our walk will be.

I also set my intentions for the day, putting it out there to the universe and the energy of the trees to help me with whatever I'm working on that day – a work task, a relationship, a personal value – and I request that it will be effortless.

Then, I begin my beautifully connected walk in the grounds perched on top of an extinct volcano – ten hectares of picturesque gardens with a mix of native and exotic plants, and many, many beautiful sky-reaching, windy, knotty, and charismatic mature trees that have been there for hundreds of years.

For me, nature has always been a sanctuary. I instantly feel grounded and calm, my vibration rises, and I find my equilibrium once more. In my twenties, I discovered the simple joy of tree-hugging, a regular practice, even if it seemed a bit unusual to others.

I also became an avid hiker and walked across Spain twice, completing the Camino de Santiago (the Frances route), walking 30km a day for thirty-two days each time. This wasn't just a long hike; it was a deeply energetic and connected journey. The well-known "ley lines" along the Camino are thought to be pathways of powerful, natural energy, fostering spiritual growth and clarity, and even offering healing and a sense of sacred exchange. Later, I discovered the formal practice of forest bathing and cleansing, which beautifully articulated what I had instinctively been drawn to all along.

Each day, I have a little chat with the trees and "fill up my cup." I call upon the energy from the trees to heal my body and keep me strong so I can live the life I am here to live. For me, this is a form of movement meditation. I use breathwork, a body scan, and focus on my needs in that moment, feeling a sense of oneness with the trees, the earth, and my surroundings.

> **"In every walk with nature one receives far more than he seeks."**
> – John Muir

I've refined this skill of calling upon the trees' energy to heal, and it truly works. I'm grateful each day for this beautiful grounding process and even more grateful for the ability to heal the pain my body has carried. The healing aspect is fascinating.

I mentally ask for the energy, visualise it, and then focus on the part of my body where I feel pain. I repeat this process three times, often asking aloud when I'm alone. For example, I might ask for the energy to heal the pain in my leg. Then, almost magically, it diminishes or disappears. I picture pushing energy into that specific area of my leg. And I can tell you, it works. Suddenly, I can continue walking without that pain.

For me, that's powerful magic. I call it magic because it's something I can't see, but I can feel it through the incredible energy of the universe. I wish I had learned this when I was experiencing chronic pain before my hip replacement. This is something different; and I really want you to try it.

> There is no doubt this practice has changed my life. Whether or not you're fully open to it, I want you to experience the pleasure and the feeling of oneness. You'll raise your vibration and likely notice physical changes within yourself.

My Morning Affirmation
(Feel free to adapt it and make it your own!)

"Hello, tree." I choose one that catches my eye, smile at it, and send it all my love. Then, I begin my walk …

I feel my feet connecting with the ground. I feel the air on my face, that light tingle on the tip of my nose. I listen to all the sounds around me and connect with each one. I take three deep, cleansing breaths in and out, feeling the air fill my lungs. And then, I speak my affirmation aloud.

"Today, is going to be a good day."

I then take some time to feel the beautiful energy from these trees.

"I am open to receiving love from the universe, and I am open to giving my love. This walk is going to be effortless, healthy, and safe. We are connected. I am protected. Peach is protected, and my babies at home are safe. We are safe, happy, and healthy."

I then take some time to just observe where I am and feel the glorious energy from these magnificent trees. I set out my intentions for the day, asking the universe and the energy of the trees to help me with whatever I'm working on that day – a work task, a relationship, a personal challenge. And yes, always affirm that it will be effortless.

    I ask the trees to heal me, both locally (my body: my knees, hip, etc.) and globally (my approachability to love, relationships, and compassion for others).

    I finish by saying again out loud, "Today is going to be a great day." Then, I walk on with the sides of my mouth curling up, in a wide, energetic, infectious smile.

> And you know something, it's very rare that I don't have a ripper day! Or what I am doing that day turns out to be effortless!

· · ·

🔗 Two: Your Daily Creation – Dreams to Reality
Shaping Your Day, Shaping Your Destiny

Remember way back at the beginning of our journey together, in *Book One: Project Clarity*? We talked about planting the seeds of intention, what you longed to have bloom in your life. Well, my friend, look how far you've come! Now, standing here on this beautiful threshold, it's time to consciously call in the magic you desire moving forward. This is about you, in your full Feminine Energetic power, shaping the landscape of your becoming.

First off, take a breath with me – a deep, glorious inhale that fills you right up. Now, just for a moment, let your inner wisdom bubble up. What do you *intend* to experience just for today? How about next week? Lean into that desire. This is how you gently allow a new habit to form. Just setting a simple intention each morning will help you weave this beautiful practice into the tapestry of your daily life.

Now, listen, I know this might feel a little weird at first; it's new, and that's okay. Totally normal. Give yourself permission for it to feel a little different at first. Just whisper to that little voice of resistance, "Hey (your loving nickname). We're just trying this on for size." Be gentle with yourself and just give it a whirl. See how it dances with your energy. These little acts of intention are like tiny, loving nudges, guiding you closer and closer to the magnificent woman you are unfolding into.

Think about it, my friend. Right here, right now, holding this book, you are a kaleidoscope of vibrant energy, armed with newfound awareness, incredible skills, and a deep connection to your own inner power. You are holding a lot more truth in the palm of your hand, aren't you now? So, see what beautiful experiences you can invite into your days. What will you whisper to the universe, declaring a pure intention that you wish to see unfolding in your brand-new world?

And, hey, life happens, right? Sometimes those bothersome energy vampires try to sneak in and dim your sparkle. When you feel that familiar tug, that drain on your precious light, how will you stand tall, rooted in your intention, and calmly but firmly say, "Not today, thank you"? How will you set your energetic boundaries and move through that with grace and unwavering self-respect?

> **"We either live with intention or exist by default."**
> – Kristin Armstrong

As I said at the beginning of these pages, there might be moments – as you courageously step away from old patterns of people-pleasing and embrace your own glorious needs – where things feel a little ... different. Relationships might shift, and you might find yourself with more precious "me-time". In those moments, how will you intentionally wrap yourself in self-compassion, setting the tone for this new chapter with gentleness and love?

Remember, your Change Experience journey of growth isn't always a straight, smooth path. Embrace the little bumps and wiggles along the way and give yourself grace, calming space, and plenty of time to feel every colourful emotion that comes with them.

You've gathered these amazing new tools, these budding superpowers, this inner strength you might not have even known was there, to see you through this. Just by showing up for yourself in these pages, you've already shed some of that old skin. So now, how will you intentionally fan the flames of this momentum? What does consciously shaping your path forward look like for the incredible multi-coloured woman you are becoming?

> Let's bring back that trusty tool we talked about – your S.M.A.R.T. goals! Setting intentions is similar. Be crystal clear, my friend. Be specific about what your heart truly wants to experience. Paint a vivid picture of your path forward.

Here is where I find these concepts to be a little mind-blowing sometimes. The incredible truth is, the laws of physics have proven that "thoughts become things". What you think about creates energy, which creates form – think about that! These thoughts of yours, yep, they become *things*. It's not just some lovely saying; brilliant minds like Mike Dooley (a New York Times bestselling author, speaker, and entrepreneur in the philosophical New Thought movement) have illuminated it through scientific study and publications, globally reaching out to people to expand our collective consciousness and understanding. (Seriously, go check him out – his by-line, "The Universe Talks", says it all! He's a total gem.)

I wholeheartedly agree with Mike, and so, I challenge you to really ponder the power of your mind in creating your reality. If your thoughts have this incredible potential, then it's time to become the magnificent gatekeeper of your mind! This is why I have been steering you to connect to your inner dialogue, so you can consciously clear out and change the narrative of any lingering negative chatter. This is your time to shift one *past-trauma-created, low-vibration self-talk conversation* at a time, to welcome thoughts and new narratives of all the good things you are calling into your life. You have this super-power now – the ability to tell those old, heavy thoughts gently but firmly, "Thank you for your company, but I'm creating a new relationship with myself here."

What might be helpful, when you have an intention that feels authentic, is to write it down. Feel the energy of your intentions on the page. And then, my beautiful friend, say them out loud. Let your own ears hear the power of your intentions. Let your voice carry those desires into the universe. And just like we've practised throughout this journey, make it a habit. This, my friend, is how you consciously sculpt the magnificent Future Self that is already within you, waiting to step out into the light.

> **"Be awake and aware of the beautiful seeds you are planting with every thought, knowing they will blossom into the experiences you desire."**
> – Maria Montessori

> There is so much light around you. Don't ever forget that.

Play with What Works for You

As you saw, I shared my daily affirmations with you in the previous pages. These have become my routine now. I am particular about what I ask for and make no exceptions. Even when I'm driving somewhere, I set an intention that it will be safe and I'll arrive at my destination safe, healthy, and happy. I know this keeps my vibration high and helps my world run smoothly.

It's neither difficult nor complicated, and you can create it as you go. Discover what works for you and give it a try. Craft words that resonate with you because if it works for me, countless others I know, and people around the world, it can work for you too. The key is thought; it needs to feel authentic to your unique style and rhythm. So, you'll need to become comfortable with this in your own way.

> So, let's remove any "ugh" feelings from this whole intention-setting thing and bring what you want straight into this moment. Start, see how you go. Play with it.

🔗 Three: Bring on "It's Possible!" Week
Unleash Your Inhibitions and Dare to Be Different

Alright, my friend, are you ready to shake things up and sprinkle a little magic into your life? I'm not just talking about a light dusting; I mean full-on confetti cannons of possibility! Let's ditch the "no's" and the "can't do's" for a week and see what glorious new experiences unfold. I dare you!

> **"Every morning, the sun rises with endless possibilities that give you endless opportunities to begin again and to create a brand-new life."**
> – Dr. Debasish Mridha

I'm challenging you in a playful way – open your mind to new possibilities like it's your latest hobby. Think of it as a week-long adventure, a treasure hunt for joy and unexpected opportunities. If you're feeling a bit resistant, a little sceptical, or even a touch stubborn (we've all been there!), that's totally fine. Consider this your personal challenge, your secret mission, if you decide to take it on (and trust me, you'll want to!).

Introducing: "It's Possible!" Week (Cue the fanfare!)

Over the next seven glorious days, each time a question arises in your mind and your knee-jerk reaction is to say, "Nope, not a chance," replace it with a bold, "It's possible!" Switch that inner chatter, flip the script, and watch the sparks fly.

For every "no" that threatens to escape your lips, swap it for a cheeky, "It could be possible ..." and let the corners of your mouth lift into a mischievous grin.

Just do it! Try something new, something that catches your interest, something that makes you think, "Hm, interesting ..." If your gut nudges you, your inner voice says, "That could be nice!" – listen attentively. Give it a go.

For one week. See how it feels. You might just stumble upon a hidden passion, a delightful surprise, or realise that the possibilities are, in fact, outrageously endless.

> Trust me on this one – you'll be doing
> a happy dance when you see, feel,
> and experience the results!

Four to Six: *The Three Pillars of Presence*
Simple Ways to Centre You

Ah, grounding! Imagine it as simply plugging yourself back into your main power source – dear Mother Earth. Just like we did in Book Two: *A New Perspective*, I'm going to give you some more simple yet highly effective techniques to use and practise.

Can you now see and truly connect to the concept that, when you're grounded, you're more present, stable, and surefooted?

> **"Be happy in the moment, that's enough. Each moment is all we need, no more."**
>
> – Mother Teresa

Here, emotional resilience becomes much easier. It becomes normal to sustain that captivating, high vibration, keeping your energy field strong and protected. This connection, honestly, feels like giving yourself a superpower.

Here's the deal, my friend – life loves to throw us those unexpected curveballs, doesn't it? Life gets busy, stress pops up out of nowhere, emotions feel overwhelming, and sometimes we pick up on other people's negative energy – it can all feel like static electricity, leaving you feeling frazzled, scattered, and totally out of sync. When you're not grounded, it's like your inner antenna isn't connected properly, making you super sensitive to all that chaotic noise. Your vibration can dip, and your energetic boundaries can become a bit leaky, letting in energies that just don't belong to you.

These new grounding techniques are like more trusty anchors. They gently guide your awareness back to your physical body and the present moment, so you can carry on in life or continue to turn the page here. When you're firmly rooted in the here and now, it's much harder for those outside stressors to pull you off course. Think of it as building a strong, solid foundation for your energetic home.

Here's why grounding is paramount for high vibration and energy protection:

🔍 **Reduces Overwhelm and Stress:** Grounding helps to gently release excess energy and calms your nervous system. When you're less stressed and more centred, your natural vibration rises, becoming more harmonious and peaceful.

🔍 **Strengthens Your Energetic Boundaries:** When you're truly present and connected to your body, you develop a stronger sense of self and your own unique energy field. This makes it easier to tell what's yours and what isn't, allowing you to create healthy boundaries and prevent that energy leakage.

🔍 **Enhances Clarity and Focus:** A grounded mind is a clear mind. When you're not lost in a whirlwind of thoughts or anxieties, you can maintain a more positive and focused state, which beautifully supports a higher vibration.

🔍 **Increases Resilience:** Just like a tree with deep, strong roots, a grounded person can weather life's storms much more effectively. When challenges come your way, you're less likely to be knocked off balance and more able to keep your equilibrium and positive energy flowing.

🔍 **Facilitates Energy Flow:** Grounding helps to release any stagnant energy and allows for a smoother, more vibrant flow of vital energy throughout your entire system. This unobstructed flow is essential for maintaining that high vibration.

Think of it this way, my friend – If you're trying to grow a beautiful, delicate flower (your high vibration), it's so much easier to do so when its roots are planted firmly in the ground. Grounding is that essential, beautiful stability for your energetic balance. You're stable, you're present, and you're far less likely to be swayed or knocked over by any external forces.

These exercises have really helped me, and my clients, and now I'd like to share them with you. These aren't just techniques; they're tools to help you reconnect with your energy, understand what that connection can do for you, and ultimately, manage those automatic behaviours that sometimes get the best of us.

> Because when you're grounded, you're balanced.
> When you're balanced, you're peaceful!
> And when you're peaceful, your senses are heightened, allowing you to listen and feel.

Four: Breathing and Body Scan
Your Instant Calm

For me, this is like an instant dose of calm. It's my go-to when I need to find my centre quickly. Here's how we do it:

Find Your Spot: You can lie down on a mat, your bed, or stand with your feet firmly on the floor. If you're standing, take your shoes and socks off – let your feet feel that direct connection to the earth.

Feel the Connection: Take a moment to become aware of every part of your body touching the surface beneath you. If you're lying down, feel your upper and lower back, your spine, arms, hands, fingers, hips, legs, knees, feet, toes, thighs, ankles, and the back of your head. If you're standing, just focus on the feeling of your feet contacting the ground.

4-7-8 Breathing: Let's incorporate the breathing technique. Breathe in through your nose for a count of 4, hold that breath for 7, and then exhale slowly through your nose for 8. Really push out all the remaining air until your lungs are completely empty. Take two or three natural breaths and then repeat this cycle three times. You can do it more if you like – four or five times – until you feel that deep sense of soothing and calming. It's like an absolute surrender.

Benefits: This exercise helps to quiet the mind, to reduce stress, and to bring you into the present moment. You'll find your heart rate slows, your thoughts become clearer, and you'll feel a wonderful sense of peace wash over you.

Make sure you fill your lungs from the bottom up, starting with your diaphragm and then the top of your lungs. Shallow breaths can make you feel dizzy, and we want this to be a grounding, not a disorienting, experience!

> **"Breath is the bridge which connects life to consciousness, which unites your body to your thoughts."**
> – Thich Nhat Hanh

Five: Fifteen Minutes of Magic

I call this "Fifteen Minutes of Magic" because that's exactly what it is. It's a beautiful way to maintain your energy equilibrium and elevate your vibration. And, honestly, who doesn't want a little magic in their day?

> **"Consciousness is only possible through change; change is only possible through movement."**
> – Aldous Huxley

If you're short on time, even five minutes can make a difference. You could even step outside your office, take your shoes off, and connect with the earth for a few moments. It's all about finding what works for you.

Get Moving: Movement is such a fantastic way to maintain and boost your energy. I recommend fifteen minutes of movement to start your day, every day. I walk every morning; it's non-negotiable for me. I love walking in nature because it really helps me to be grounded. If you can, take your shoes off and let your toes feel the earth – the grass or the sand, whatever's beneath your feet. Feel that connection as you walk.

Mini Body Scan: While you're walking and connecting with Mother Earth, do a mini scan of your body. Start from your head and work your way down to your toes. What does your head feel like? Are your shoulders tense or relaxed? Call it out, either in your mind or out loud if you can. Go through your ribs, down your spine, to your hips. Are they balanced? How do your thighs, knees, calf muscles, ankles, heels, and toes feel? Just notice and acknowledge.

Benefits: Being in nature calms your nervous system, connects you to the earth's energy, and helps you release tension. The body scan brings you into greater awareness of your physical state, allowing you to address any areas of tightness or discomfort. You might feel more energised, more centred, and more connected to yourself and the world around you.

> Oh! And ... first light or when there's a full moon are extra special times to do this.

Six: Raise Your Vibe with Tunes

This one's all about connecting your vibration to music and sound. Your vibration is part of your energy field, and the higher the frequency, the lighter and happier you feel. You're more open to clarity, love, happiness, and joy.

Tune In: Put on some music that speaks to you. Feel the vibration of the music in your body. Do a body scan. Then, move! Stand still, sway, dance – whatever feels right in the moment. If you feel comfortable, hum along. Feel that vibration flow through you.

> **"Music gives a soul to the universe, wings to the mind, flight to the imagination, and life to everything."**
> – Plato

Express Yourself: I have playlists on Spotify that I love to dance to. Sometimes I sing; sometimes I howl at the moon! I might grab a wooden spoon and have a little concert for myself. It's all about getting that energy out and connecting with the vibration of my voice.

Benefits: Music has the power to shift your mood, uplift your spirits, and raise your vibration. By moving your body and expressing yourself through sound, you release stagnant energy and invite in feelings of joy, freedom, and connection. You might feel more creative, more inspired, and more aligned with your true self.

Could You Give It a Go?

As you navigate your own journey of change, I wholeheartedly encourage you to just give these techniques a trial run. Observe yourself – what do you notice, how do you feel? Then, see if you can have another go and observe again. And then another!

Being committed might take some practice, which I know can be tough to fit into your life – I get it! So, make a diary note if you must. It's only when you genuinely see and feel the benefits of these practices that you will want to keep going.

And when you do, you'll realise that they're like your new superpowers – a golden ticket to stop those automatic behaviours and reconnect with your inner strength.

> If the wooden spoon and singing out loud isn't your thing, that's totally okay! Just hum along to the music. Don't be embarrassed about your voice – everyone can sing in their own way. Find songs that make you feel good and use that as your connection to pure joy.

Capture that feeling. That is what it feels like to own your energy, big time.

21. Remember When

Connecting to Your Core Wounds – In a Liberated Way
How Unmet Needs Become Your Guiding Light

Alright, here's where I connect you back to the first exercise in Book One: *Project Clarity*. I asked you to place your hand on your heart and read the following text aloud to see what came up. I hope you wrote your answers in your journal. Maybe you can revisit them briefly? I asked you to consider six questions about what you longed for from your parents. Here it is again for you:

Your Core Wounds Exercise

1. What's one thing you received from Dad that you didn't truly want?
2. What's one thing you received from Mum that you didn't really want?
3. What's one thing you longed for from Dad, but never received?
4. What's one thing you longed for from Mum, but never received?

5. What overarching theme or feeling connects those words (i.e., rejection)?

6. What are ten different single words that reflect what you needed back then? What did your heart honestly yearn for?

Now, I want to share what this meant for me. If you've lost your answers from the first exercise or don't remember them, that's okay. Read these out loud to yourself, then carry on and look at my answers. This might help you connect with your truth in these questions or help you realise that what you went through is more common than you thought.

Here are my answers

1. What's one thing you received from Dad that you didn't truly want? **The sense I was never enough.**

2. What's one thing you received from Mum that you didn't really want? **The sense that I could never trust people.**

3. What's one thing you longed for from Dad, but never received? **Acceptance.**

4. What's one thing you longed for from Mum, but never received? **Authenticity.**

5. What overarching theme or feeling connects those words? **Invalidation.**

6. What are ten (or more) different single words that reflect what you needed back then?
   - **Safety:** What my heart honestly yearned for.
   - **Security:** I didn't feel safe in my own home.
   - **Acknowledgement:** I didn't feel seen for who I really was.
   - **Honesty:** I felt like we were all fake, keeping up appearances.
   - **Kindness:** I felt like being shamed was how I was treated for any wrongdoing.
   - **Connection:** I grew up without my parents. They worked all the time.

- *Peace:* I witnessed so much aggravation and turmoil, fights between my parents and family that frightened me.
- *Understanding:* I was scolded, then given the silent treatment when I did something wrong.
- *Clarity:* I was punished when I didn't know what I had done wrong.
- *Stability:* I had to leave home when I was twelve and was sent to boarding school.
- *Nurturing:* When I was sick, I was given all the wrong foods (sweet, rich, fatty foods).
- *Respect:* There were never any boundaries or respect for my space.
- *Direction:* I was never taught any life rules.
- *Structure:* I was never taught any discipline, other than to live in fear of being shamed.
- *Support:* When I needed help, there was none.
- *Validation:* I was gaslit to believe the problem was always my fault.
- *Encouragement:* I was made fun of and ridiculed when I was trying my best.
- *Guidance:* I was never taught how to do anything; I had to work it out for myself.

Sharing this vulnerable part of my journey feels essential to me. It shines a light on the very roots of complex trauma, and it's a powerful reminder of my commitment not to be defined by past challenges.

All those missing pieces from my childhood? I've woven them into the very fabric of how I live now. They guide my personal love-myself-actions, deepening the love I have for myself in general and strengthening the boundaries I hold dear. They also shape how I connect with others in every area of my life. I hope you can see how I've transformed those unmet needs into sources of immense personal power.

> **"The whole point of seeing through something is to see something through it."**
> — C. S. Lewis

Embracing these needs and holding my boundaries fiercely allows me to move through life with grace. It helps me make choices that bring balance, peace, and true joy. And most importantly, it's the foundation for keeping my energy clear and bright, and my vibration resonating at a high, harmonious level.

When you see your own experiences written down (after you have said to yourself, "*This really sucked, didn't it?!*"), I believe you'll begin to simply appreciate your own strength and resilience. And you'll see how those unmet needs can become your guiding light, a way to protect and nurture your own precious energy.

Trust me, when I read these responses of my own, it sometimes still makes my eyes well up. But it's not too long before a warm feeling of pride and validation that raises my vibration again. It's humbling, and it's all part of who I am.

> Can you see what I am saying here, my friend? I'm still here, holding your hand.

Liberated Connection – A Future Defined by You

22. What's the Vibe Now?

You're Here!
Present, Reflecting on Your Transformation

Alright, let's take a moment. You are now in the final stages of this third and final book in the series. Three whole volumes of deep exploration completed – you've journeyed through some deep stuff in these books, right? – that, my friend, is a monumental amount of self-discovery! Wow. You've unlocked and bravely looked at the shadows, hugged that inner, beautifully bold, little girl who kept trying to get your attention, and stood tall as the amazing woman you are today. Superb effort! All with a nod to the even more beautiful you in your Future Self.

So, shall we get on to a pragmatic view of what life *feels* like right now? Grab your journal and take some time to reflect. And, by now, I think you know the drill: Read the questions out loud, and then read what you have written out loud to yourself.

> **"Happiness is when what you think, what you say, and what you do are in harmony."**
> – Mahatma Gandhi

This is your gift of connection, remember.

Let's Do a Little Check-In.

1. Reflect on how the insights from these books are manifesting in your daily life right now. In what specific ways do you notice these lessons influencing your everyday actions? Do your current actions feel aligned with your core values? Are you observing any subtle shifts in those automatic behaviours? Can you sense the link between what you've learned and how you're living today?

2. Reflect on situations that usually trigger you. Right now, are you noticing those triggers earlier before they fully take over? And when you do face them, how are you intentionally choosing to respond in a way that feels different, more in line with your growth? Also, in your interactions, are you more aware of the possibility of being gaslit, and how does this awareness affect your sense of self-trust and your connection to your own reality?

3. Bring your awareness to your relationship with food and drink as it is right now. Do you notice a greater sense of control and conscious choice in these areas? Are you actively staying present with your emotions, allowing yourself to feel them instead of reaching for food or drink to numb or distract? What does this deeper connection with your feelings feel like in your body and in your daily choices?

4. Reflect on your ability to create space for your emotions today. Are you finding moments to acknowledge them, even the tough ones, and allowing them to exist without judgement? How does your current capacity to be with your emotions reflect that strength and self-acceptance? What does this new openness to your emotional world reveal about your journey so far?

What Does Three Months from Now Look Like?

I want you to stretch your mind and imagine how your world may look and feel as you grow, practise your new skills, and make the changes you desire. Then, think ahead and let's have a look at the next three months. What does life look like for you, and what new things are you planning to bring into your life?

1. Imagine your Future Self three months from now. What are her key qualities? Does this vision feel truly genuine, a natural progression of who you are becoming? When you connect with this future version of yourself, what emotions arise? What is it like to fully embody her essence?

2. What specific changes have you intentionally made in your daily routine to maintain consistently high energy levels? How have you prioritised restorative sleep, actively reduced your stress, embraced a nourishing and balanced diet, and incorporated regular physical activity to support your body? Reflect on the combined impact of these changes. How does this newfound energetic balance feel to you now, both physically and emotionally? What noticeable differences do you see in how you show up and navigate life?

3. Looking ahead, how will you actively live out your values? Picture a specific moment when your actions reflect these values. What's the internal experience of living in such alignment? What does that authentic life feel like? Can you sense that connection to your core beliefs in your future day-to-day?

4. Imagine a moment when you face a challenge. Now that you have all these new skills, how do you approach it? How does it feel to use your practised skills and grounding techniques? Have these tools become easier to use when things feel unsteady? How do you feel about doing more practice and being kind to yourself if you don't get it right every time? (Don't worry; I still practise mine even now.) What does it feel like to know that you

have these resources within you now? What does that connection to your inner resilience feel like?

5. Thinking about your emotional landscape with perspective, how would you describe your ability to navigate your feelings with more flexibility and understanding? Think about a time when a boundary needed to be set. Even if it felt a little shaky at first, how did you stand firm in your need for the boundary? How has working on setting boundaries become more natural and less daunting, helping you connect to your own emotional health and needs?

6. Picture a situation now where you need to set a boundary. How do you confidently and kindly assert yourself, saying a "firm but loving no"? What's the feeling of empowerment and self-respect that comes with this? Can you feel the connection to your own needs and the ease with which you honour them in this future scenario?

7. Three months from now, you'll have created space from chaos and the energy vampire. Suppose a moment of loneliness or self-doubt arises, leading you to question your decision (even though you know it was correct). How will you recognise and validate your own feelings? What specific steps will you take to support yourself and reaffirm your choice?

8. What does joy look like in your daily life? Describe some of the small, simple pleasures that bring a smile to your face and lift your spirits. What are those moments that create a deep sense of happiness and contentment?

9. What does inner peace feel like within you? Describe the sensations, thoughts, and overall state of being. How important has cultivating this peace become for you now as you look towards the future? How does it feel when you connect with the possibility of experiencing this consistent inner peace? (What was the

first thing that came to mind when you read this last sentence out loud?)

These are good things to think about, right? Let them simmer in that brilliant mind of yours. Because you know what? Straight lines in life? Nah, that's not for us. Life is going to be life, with all its crunchy imperfections. Things will still pop out of a bush and give you a fright, and that's okay. When they do, these new skills you have to hold yourself will be right there, ready to go. Emotional storms – yep, you've got this; no more losing yourself and reaching for a bottle or a packet of something processed and numbing. Your darkest, most shameful memories of your Former Self – no more pushing them into a dusty corner! They're part of your awareness now.

Seriously, talking to yourself about this stuff? It builds a real connection. Embrace the feeling of authenticity, self-empathy, trust, and knowing that even when you stumble and make a mistake, things are still going smoothly. You can breathe through it and be okay because you've learned something new about yourself. Haven't you?

What does it feel like when you're truly living by those authentic commitments you've made? Grab a pen and jot it down. Get it out of your head and onto the page.

> You are seriously getting good at this! You've got this in the bag.

Six Months from Now ...

Let's do the same. Really imagine what life will be like for you after six more months of developing your new skills, living according to your values, catching yourself before you are triggered, and living the life you want. Can you picture how you believe life will be for me?

> Even if you only glance at them, let these questions gently plant a seed for more thought.

1. Connect with your Future Self more clearly. What tangible changes have you made in your life? What knowledge have you gained so far? When making changes, what has felt natural, and what has required more effort? What fundamental values have now come into focus for you?

2. Reflect on how you now recognise gaslighting. How easily can you identify those attempts? What is your internal feeling when it occurs? Are you better able to stay centred and manage your emotional responses with more clarity?

3. Reflect on your friends and family bonds. How easily (or with mindful effort) are you setting and keeping your boundaries? And what is the emotional climate like because of it? How does it feel to honour your own needs within those relationships?

4. We all have those people in our lives whose energy can sometimes feel overwhelming. Six months from now, after spending time with someone like that, how are your energy levels? What nurturing practices have you adopted to restore your vitality? Are you finding it easier to create the necessary space with this person, or is that still a delicate area you're navigating with care?

5. Look around you in your mind's eye. Who are the bright spots in your life now? Who is resonating with your journey? Who is also actively working on their own growth and empowerment? Whose presence consistently validates your choices and makes you feel truly seen for who you are becoming?

6. Now, let's gently turn that focus inward. How are you truly showing up for your own needs? What does it feel like to prioritise your health, especially before seeking external approval – particularly from those whose opinions once carried weight? What's it like to honour your own desires and needs first?

7. Alright, honestly, life will still have its moments, won't it? When something now triggers you, where do you find yourself landing

emotionally? How much do you trust that powerful "Choice Point" within you – that moment when you consciously decide how to respond to that trigger with your evolving self, intentionally choosing to live by your values?

8. And if you find yourself caught in an emotional storm, what specific steps are you now taking to navigate those automatic patterns around food and drink? What is it like to recognise and gently redirect yourself to something else to soothe you after an emotional stumble?

9. Imagine a moment of celebration, and the thought of a drink comes to mind. How does that feel now? What is the sensation of having greater control, of setting healthy boundaries around social drinking, so you remain true to your own intentions rather than being influenced by others?

10. What's your experience of trusting yourself more deeply now? How does it feel to genuinely listen to the voice of your intuition, of your body, and your energy? What is the sensation of confidently taking action that aligns with your truth, knowing that you are your own best guide, regardless of external pressures or opinions?

11. How are you applying your grounding skills now? Are they becoming an instinctive part of your toolkit, a dependable way to find your centre? How do they assist you in maintaining your inner balance, easing any anxieties, and gently quieting those repetitive thoughts that once filled your mind?

12. And that beautiful, compassionate connection with your inner self … How are you nurturing that empathetic witness within? How are those loving conversations with your Inner Child unfolding? (Honestly, this is a continuous journey. Even now, those moments of newfound connection with my own Inner Child are so valuable.)

13. In six months, how will acceptance genuinely feel to you? As you look back on your journey, how fully are you embracing every stumble and perceived mistake as a worthwhile lesson, valuing the insight each one provides? Can you reflect and see how your life's path, with all its twists and turns, has led you to this moment with a deeper understanding of yourself? How completely are you accepting who you are – including those parts that have borne the burden of past challenges – and recognising what you've been through? In six months, what will freedom from your past be like?

Pause for a moment to imagine what your life might look like in six months. Sit with this thought and ask yourself, "What's my life going to be like?" (Remember, all these thoughts generate energy around you.) It's like turning on the headlights on a dark road and paying attention to that path. That's your inner GPS, guiding you to the skills you might need to improve. It's another way of setting intentions for your greater good. This helps you connect with your destination with clarity and perspective. Think about the more skilled, more resilient version of yourself that's emerging. This is all part of your incredible evolution.

> **"The only person you are destined to become is the person you decide to be."**
> – Ralph Waldo Emerson

These questions and reflections might take some time. So, don't panic or get overwhelmed. You can ask yourself the questions and just let them soak in and percolate. You might want to put these questions out into the universe and see what happens. Regardless of what you decide, just by reading them aloud to yourself, you've created a connection. And through that connection, my friend, change can happen. Maybe not today or tomorrow, but it will come if you believe in it and want it to.

In Twelve Months ...

In twelve months, your journey on this Change Experience should be pretty colourful. Your life will be different, no doubt. Suppose you are practising your skills, paying attention to living by your values, setting clear boundaries, and managing your emotions so you don't get thrown around so much when you experience a trigger. In that case, the world should feel different, in a positively refreshing way.

Ok, here is our challenge. Go back and ask yourself some of the previous questions, but this time, repeat these contemplations through the eyes of a wiser, more capable, more skilful woman. Hmm, interesting, huh?

When you stop and think about it, life will be very different in twelve months, right? If you are consistently working on small shifts, such as increasing your awareness, connecting with your core Inner Child, healing your wounds, and better managing your needs within healthy boundaries, thoughts about energy drainers probably won't feel as significant. Instead, it will shift to recognising who naturally takes a role in your life to honour your energy. Your inner circle in twelve months will surely be different. And, hey, if that picture is a little fuzzy right now, no worries! It'll come.

Transformation often means our tribe shifts, and that's okay. You'll have new connections in your life at that point, which will bring joy and happiness in a whole different manner. Be open to the possibilities and trust that the right people will come into your life as you continue to grow. Connecting with others who share your values? That's a beautiful thing.

In twelve months, your Liberation Toolbox will be your essential resource for nurturing your home-grown peace and joy. It's a space to check in with yourself and ask, "Do I trust myself, always?" (That must be non-negotiable by now.)

> **"The longest journey you will ever take is the one to yourself."**
> – Terri Guillemets

[?] Do you show empathy towards your inner self, your past self, and view these experiences through a compassionate lens?

[?] Do you use your breathwork to manage your emotions and anxiety, creating space for you to go through life with more happiness?

[?] Do you see every stumble and mistake as a learning opportunity and feel grateful for what it has taught you?

[?] Do you see how your life has unfolded with more acceptance and understanding of your past?

[?] Do you accept who you are and all the parts of you that have suffered due to past challenges, and take what has happened to you? Then, use that as your line in the sand, the turning point in your life to make a change.

[?] Can you acknowledge you are no longer a victim? You are a woman with a new vision and a much broader connection to yourself, which gives you the freedom to change. Freedom to move forward as a more liberated, authentic woman.

Your Role in This

Now, your journal is your companion and best friend to support you through this Change Experience. Write, read, and speak your words aloud. Take your time while you have a little chat with your Future Self about what things look like in three, six, and twelve months. What is she telling you about life on the other side of making these conscious choices? Just be still for a moment and listen. The answer will bubble up. And then, you know what to do – write it down. And speak your truth aloud.

> **"The best way to predict the future is to create it."**
> – Peter Drucker

You can even take your journal and head to the mirror, look yourself in those beautiful eyes, and say those words aloud. Own them. And then see how that feels. It might feel a little weird, unsettling, or even titillating. Please go and see what it feels like to look yourself in the eye when you talk about the changes afoot in your life and the beautiful evolution before you.

• • •

On We Go ...

As you step forward, remember those wise words we explored way back when. When life throws a little ... spice your way, try on a new lens. See those challenges not as roadblocks but as juicy opportunities for growth. Seriously! Every hurdle, every little stumble, is just a chance for you to learn something new about yourself, to evolve, and to become even more resilient. Think of it as the universe giving you a little nudge to look inward and unleash even more of your inner strength.

And, hey, remember you're not alone in this human experience. We all face our moments of "ugh". Recognising that struggle is part of the deal can make you feel more connected, more ... normal. We're all in this beautiful, messy journey together.

And, come on, remember to tap into your inner superhero! (This is not to be cheesy but to affirm that stories of significant transformation exist for a reason.) Remember the Wonder Woman analogy? Think about how those amazing heroes face adversity head-on. They don't shrink away; they rise to the occasion. Who's *your* inner superhero? Channel that energy! Challenges are what make heroes, my darling friend. They're what make *you* even more magnificent.

And when things feel tough, zoom out a little. Think about that incredible Future Self you're building. How will overcoming *this* current bump in the road benefit her? That Change Experience you've been navigating? It's all about taking the long view, about nurturing the needs of that future, and even more empowered you.

You've got this, my friend. You are strong, you are capable, and you are constantly evolving. Keep shining that beautiful light, and know that every step you take, every intention you set, is guiding you towards the radiant future you deserve. Now go out there and create some magic!

This is your time. This is you defining yourself. This is you taking the reins and deciding how you want to live, how you want to feel. Self-love, peace, joy, feeling like you are worthy of all of this, is within you. Now, just reach in and grab hold of it.

> And just whisper to yourself,
> "Thank you for being present."

23.
The Triumph of You

You've Done It!
Your Next Chapter – Living Your Change Experience

My friend, look at you! You've put in a massive amount of time and effort to follow your unique Change Experience through to the end. Seriously, give yourself a massive hug right now, because I am absolutely beaming that you're here, reading these final words. You didn't just pick up some light reading; you dove deep, you faced the tough stuff, and you *finished*. That's HUGE! Your incredible Future Self is already sending you a massive high-five.

> **"Courage is the price that life exacts for granting peace."**
> – Amelia Earhart

I want to take a real moment to acknowledge the sheer effort you've poured into this. The courage it took to look into those hidden corners, the commitment you made to your own beautiful becoming – that's not small stuff. This wasn't a gentle stroll through a field of daisies, was it? This was real, honest work, and you, my magnificent friend, navigated it. You emerged on the other side, undoubtedly a more knowing, more resilient woman, and frankly, a woman who is now unstuck!

The Power of Forward Motion

Now that you're actively working on removing the barriers that kept you stuck and are consciously trusting yourself – your confidence in your ability to make change can genuinely grow.

As you heal and fully acknowledge that you are no longer a victim, a vast new capacity opens up within you. This safe place you've created enables you to step into what making change actually means. Remember, confidence is built through trying – it's about giving it a red-hot crack and seeing what happens! See how your confidence grows with even the smallest action, and remember to embrace all the crunchy little bits of imperfection along the way.

So, go on, how about trying a little change on for size? What have you really got to lose?

This is the Law of Attraction finally winking at you. As the wise Mike Dooley always says, "Thoughts become things, so you really have to choose the good ones!" Let that sink in: You've got the power to shape your reality, one thought at a time.

Now, as you step into this next chapter, keep that intention-setting muscle strong. Plant both feet firmly in the good vibes camp, and trust in the power of all those insights and actions you've committed to. They will bloom, sister. That's not just wishful thinking; that's the universe saying, "Okay, I see you, and I'm on your team." Just like I am.

You're amazing.

Fleur Elizabeth

P.s – Tell me honestly, have you ever shown up for yourself this much before?

Now, go be you!

Appendix and References

I.
Appendix: Your Living Blueprint

Practices for Ongoing Transformation

Alright, my champion woman of the ages! You've reached the end of this part of our journey together, and honestly, my heart is swelling with pride for the incredible work you've done. This isn't just about reading words; it's about cracking open your own inner landscape and having a good, honest look around. That takes guts, pure and simple.

Think of this little appendix as your personal treasure map. You've gathered so many tools and insights within these pages; these questions are just the key to unlock those treasures and positively integrate them into the vibrant tapestry of your life.

> **"Become who you are by learning who you are."**
> – Pindar

So, grab your favourite pen and your journal once more, settle into a comfy spot, and let's dig a little deeper, shall we?

Let's Begin

1. **Your Next Steps: Planting Seeds of Change.** Let's get down to brass tacks, in that lovely, thoughtful way we do. You've unearthed so much about what you truly desire. Now, how will that translate into the real world?

2. **Love and Connection:** Looking at your relationships – the ones that lift you and the ones that might need a little recalibrating – what's one brave step you're ready to take to nurture deeper authenticity and healthier boundaries in those connections? What might you say or do differently to honour your own needs while still cherishing those you hold dear?

3. **Work and Purpose:** Considering your vocational life, that space where you contribute your unique magic to the world – what's one intentional shift you can make, however small, to bring more alignment with your values and create a healthier rhythm in your days? How can you infuse more of *you* into what you do?

4. **Your Amazing Body:** When it comes to your physical health and those choices around nourishment and movement, what's one loving action you can commit to this week that honours your body's wisdom and supports your energy? No punishing regimes here, just genuine care.

5. **Your Brilliant Mind:** Nurturing that precious headspace of yours – what's one consistent practice, even if it's just for five minutes a day, that you'll weave into your routine to cultivate more calm, clarity, and self-compassion? What will be your go-to for those moments when the inner critic gets a little too loud?

6. **Moving Your Body, Moving Your Soul:** Thinking about how you choose to move and energise your body – what's one joyful way you can incorporate more movement into your life that feels less like a chore and more like a celebration of what your body can do? What feels genuinely good?

7. **The Beautiful Dance of Mistakes:** Because let's be real, we're human, and wobbles happen! What's one learned and self-compassionate response you'll consciously choose the next time you stumble or feel like you've taken a step back? How will you remind yourself that this is all part of the messy, beautiful process?

Your Leadership in Your Change Experience

You are the CEO of your own transformation, my friend. You've taken the reins. Now, let's reflect on the incredible leader you are becoming.

1. **Your Guiding Light:** Think about that powerful connection you've forged with your Future Self. How will you continue to tap into her emotional maturity and let her vision fuel your daily choices and actions? What message does she have for you right now?

2. **Your Inner Compass:** You've learned so much about your values. How will you actively use these as your compass, guiding your decisions and ensuring you're living a life that genuinely resonates with your authentic self? What will be your non-negotiables moving forward?

3. **Your Energetic Boundaries:** You've bravely explored the art of setting healthy boundaries. How will you continue to honour your precious energy and create space for what simply nourishes you? While also pragmatically (or firmly) protecting yourself from what drains you?

4. **Your Confidence Blooming:** Reflect on how your confidence in your ability to create lasting change has shifted throughout this journey. What's one small but significant action you can take this week that will further solidify that belief in yourself and your power to shape your life?

5. **Navigating the Storms:** You've gained incredible tools for handling emotional storms. How will you consciously put these

into practice when those inevitable turbulent moments arise, remembering to be kind and patient with yourself in the process?

6. **Your Ongoing Evolution:** Change is a dance, not a destination. How will you stay open to the ongoing evolution within you, embracing the unexpected twists and turns with curiosity and self-compassion? What does it feel like to have the capacity to make change effortlessly?

・・・

II.
Appendix: Your Future Self, Reimagined

Returning to Your Vision with New Eyes
Defining Your Liberated Becoming

As you reach the final pages of our journey together in this series, I wanted to offer you a sweet invitation to revisit a space we first explored at the very beginning, in Book One: *Project Clarity*. Remember when we paused and asked, "Who is your Future Self?" At that time, it was a seed of potential, a vision you held perhaps with a mix of hope for the possibilities and apprehension of the unknown.

Now, having journeyed through these pages, having bravely befriended the tender parts of yourself, and having refined a deeper understanding of your inner landscape, I invite you to ask that question again. Look at it with the emotional maturity you've gathered, the strength you've unearthed, and the compassion you now hold for all that you are. Perhaps the woman you envision now has even clearer contours, a deeper resonance, and a keener sense of self-acceptance.

Take a moment, my friend, and find your favourite journal. Allow yourself the quiet space to once again dream and define who this future version of you is. I have included

"The unexamined life is not worth living."
– Socrates

the questions once again for you to ponder. What does she embody? What wisdom does she carry? What kind of life does she live? And as you fill those pages with your heartfelt reflections, please, as always, read your words aloud. Let the sound of your own voice carry this vision, solidifying the beautiful transformation that is already unfolding within you. This time, may you hear not just a dream, but the powerful echo of the woman you are becoming.

I hope you enjoy revisiting this process.

Questions to Ask Yourself

Who Is She?

1. Imagine the woman you are becoming – the woman who has embraced growth, navigated challenges, and blossomed through transformation. What does she look like? What details do you notice about her appearance – her hair, her style, the light in her eyes?

2. Envision the environment where your Future Self lives. Describe the area, her home – is it a cosy place, a warm space filled with life? What are the immediate surroundings like? And as you picture her there, what does her physical presence tell you?

3. Take a moment to consider her sensory world. What subtle scents do you associate with your Future Self? Is it a familiar perfume, the invigorating freshness of nature, the comforting warmth of her home? What does her personal atmosphere evoke?

4. Observe your Future Self moving through her day. What is her posture like? How is she showing up in the world? What is her overall presence? What energy does she carry? How does she carry herself – with grounded confidence, fluid grace, effortless ease?

5. Envision the tapestry of connections your Future Self nurtures. What are her relationships like at home, perhaps with beloved fur babies who bring her joy? How does she connect with colleagues in her professional life? What is the depth and quality of her friendships? How does she engage with her wider community?

6. What kind of love beautifully weaves through your Future Self's life? Consider all its forms – romantic love, the cherished bonds

of family and friends, and the unconditional affection from her fur babies, if she has them.

7. How does your Future Self cherish her own company? What are her favourite ways to relax, recharge her spirit, and enjoy the peacefulness of her personal space?

8. Consider the moments when your Future Self is completely herself, behind closed doors, without pretence. What brings her private joy and allows her unfiltered, whole self to shine when no one else is watching?

Her Journey

1. What fulfilling path has your Future Self chosen for her work or life's dedication? What ignites her passion and brings her a deep sense of purpose in how she contributes her unique gifts to the world?

2. Reflect on the milestones your Future Self has celebrated, both the grand achievements and the quiet personal victories. What accomplishments fill her with a sense of pride and validation?

3. Envision your Future Self embracing challenges with a "mistakes are good" mindset. How does she approach each misstep not as a negative but as an opportunity for deeper understanding? How does she use her skills and these experiences to propel her forward? What is her resilient attitude towards imperfection?

4. Even the most luminous journeys include moments of learning. What setbacks or perceived "barriers" has your Future Self navigated? (Remember the values conflicts.) And, more importantly, what newfound know-how and invaluable growth has she extracted from those experiences? Remember, these are powerful stepping stones on her path.

Her Evolution

1. Tune into the inner dialogue of your Future Self. What kind and empowering conversations does she have with herself? What are her go-to affirmations or self-supporting beliefs? What is the tone of her inner voice – is it consistently kind, warm, and deeply encouraging, allowing her authenticity to be honoured?

2. Picture your Future Self navigating her emotional world with self-awareness and grace. How does she listen to the messages her emotions offer and communicate to her? How does she understand and regulate her emotions, without being overwhelmed by echoes of the past? How does she create a safe inner space to soothe herself and respond to challenging situations with calm clarity?

3. Imagine your Future Self moving through her life anchored in unwavering self-trust. What does this deep knowing look like in her decisions and actions? How does she intuitively listen to and honour her gut feelings? What is the perceptive sense of security that comes with this self-trust?

4. Envision your Future Self moving through her life completely free from the grip of guilt and the influence of manipulation. What does she look like when her choices are genuinely her own, no longer driven by a sense of obligation to fulfil others' needs at her own expense? How does she carry herself when she is no longer acting out of a deep-seated feeling of not being "good enough" and instead acts from a place of inherent worth and self-respect? What is the feeling of this newfound autonomy and self-assuredness?

5. Envision your Future Self living with healthy boundaries that wisely protect her energy and consciously prioritise her own needs and balance. What does this look like in her daily

interactions and the choices she makes? How does she communicate these boundaries with both confidence and grace?

Her Know-How

1. Imagine your Future Self looking back at her journey with learned empathy and deep understanding for all she has navigated. What does it look like for her to truly see and acknowledge her own pain and the weight of the difficult circumstances she faced? How has she extended forgiveness to herself for any shame she carried and for the choices she made while contending with life challenges and trauma? What is the feeling of far-reaching self-compassion and self-forgiveness that flows from her?

2. Envision your Future Self radiating a deep sense of inner security and self-validation. What does it feel like for her to no longer seek external approval or validation from others? What is the liberating sense of self-acceptance and inherent worth that shines from within her as she confidently values herself and lives authentically?

3. Imagine your Future Self having embraced her past with acceptance. What does it look like for her to acknowledge her experiences without the weight of resentment or lingering pain? How does she carry her history with grace rather than viewing it as a burden? How has she found peace with her story and nurtured enduring joy in her present?

Her Truth

1. Picture your Future Self immersed in a moment of pure, unadulterated joy. What is she doing that makes her heart sing? Who is she sharing this moment with? What are the specific details – the sights, sounds, and feelings – that illuminate her from the inside out? What does joy physically feel like within her body?

2. Imagine your Future Self living in a state of sweet inner and outer peace. How does she show up in the world, and what does this feel like in her everyday existence? What shifts in perspective or circumstances have refined this radical new sense of peace? How does she navigate life's inevitable challenges while maintaining this gentle state?

3. What does it truly mean for your Future Self to deeply and unconditionally love herself? What are the tangible ways she demonstrates this new human experience? What does it look like with her thoughts, actions, and the choices she makes? What does this new feeling of love feel like for her?

4. Then, imagine your Future Self in total ease with the beauty of self-love and confidently meeting her own needs. What does it feel like for her to be fully capable of nurturing and caring for herself, without relying on others to fill that space? What is the experience of being alone, yet feeling completely whole and at peace within her own company, free from the pang of loneliness? What does this self-contained sense of love and belonging feel like?

Her Messages to You

1. Looking back with clarity and a new perspective of your Future Self, what message of unconditional raw and real love, insightful understanding, and gentle healing would she offer to the younger version of you (your Former Self or Inner Child) who experienced such deep hurt? What kind words of compassion and essential truths would she want her to know and embrace?

2. Imagine your wise and compassionate Future Self sitting right in front of you in this present moment. What soothing yet powerful words of discernment does she have to share about your Change Experience? What would she say to offer reassurance,

provide guidance, and illuminate your path forward from where you are right now?

> The vision you are creating here is you, the connected, liberated you!

···

A Final Hug and a Light Nudge

Ciao Ciao, my friend. Take a deep breath and acknowledge just how far you've come. I have said it before, and I will say it again – this journey of change isn't always a straight line. There will be moments of exhilaration and moments of feeling like you're wading through treacle. *That's perfectly normal.* Be patient with yourself. Celebrate every tiny victory. Normalise the stumbles. And remember that the most profound and lasting transformations take time, tenderness, bucket loads of compassion and tone of trust – in good yourself.

> **"Maybe, if you put your disbelief aside, roll up your sleeves, take some risks, and totally go for it, you'll wake up one day and realise you're living the kind of life you used to be jealous of."**
>
> – Jen Sincero

You *have* the strength within you. You *have* the know-how. You *have* the courage.

Keep showing up for yourself, one brave step at a time. The path ahead is yours to create, and I have no doubt you'll fill it with your own unique brand of feminine energy, brilliance, and joy.

And let your light shine, shine, shine!

III.
References and Research

Hypervigilance. (n.d.). Wikipedia.

Patel, D. (2019, May 8). Ways to Attract Good Energy Today and Every Day. *The Entrepreneur blog posts.*

Nash, J. (2018, January 5). How to Set Healthy Boundaries & Build Positive Relationships. *Positive Psychology blog post.*

Li, Q. (2018). *Shinrin-Yoku: The Japanese Art of Forest Bathing.* Penguin Books.

[Acceptance and Commitment Therapy, Motivational Interviewing, DBT, Emotional Focus Therapy, Dialectical Behavioural Therapy]. [Online resources].

Fletcher, T. (n.d.). *Trauma Series.* YouTube.

Koosis, L. A. (2024, June 25). The Science of Affirmations: The Brain's Response To Positive Thinking.

www.ingramcontent.com/pod-product-compliance
Lightning Source LLC
Chambersburg PA
CBHW071955070526
44583CB00015B/1204